£30·00

D0146232

Local government and Thatcherism

Hugh Butcher, Ian G. Law,
Robert Leach, and Maurice Mullard

Routledge
London and New York

First published 1990
by Routledge
11 New Fetter Lane, London EC4P 4EE

Simultaneously published in the USA and Canada
by Routledge
a division of Routledge, Chapman and Hall, Inc.
29 West 35th Street, New York, NY 10001

©1990 H. Butcher, I. G. Law, R. Leach M. Mullard.

Typeset by LaserScript Limited, Mitcham, Surrey.
Printed and bound in Great Britain by
Mackays of Chatham PLC, Chatham, Kent

British Library Cataloguing in Publication Data
Local government and Thatcherism.
   1. Great Britain.   Local government.   Policies of government
   I. Butcher, Hugh
   352.041

   ISBN 0-415-03211-3
   ISBN 0-415-04430-8 (pb.)

Library of Congress Cataloging in Publication Data

Local government and Thatcherism / by Hugh Butcher . . . [et al.].
      p. cm.
   ISBN 0-415-03211-3. — ISBN 0-415-04430-8 (pbk.)
   1. Local government—Great Britain. 2. Conservatism—Great Britain.
   3. Thatcher, Margaret. I. Butcher, Hugh.
JS3095 1990
352.041—dc20

                                                        89-10907
                                                        CIP

Contents

Chapter one

Introduction

During the last decade the three Conservative administrations under the leadership of Mrs Thatcher have sought a radical transformation of local government. As far as the New Right is concerned, local government legislation presented to parliament at the end of the 1980s symbolizes the final stages of the Thatcherite attempt to break the monopoly of the Town Halls. In contrast, the advocates of public participation in the control of collective provision view the Thatcher Revolution as fatally weakening local democracy and destroying the fabric of public services.

The election of Mrs Thatcher in 1979 heralded a bid to roll back the paternalist and interventionist state, to reduce the burden of public expenditure and taxation and to increase choice and responsibility for the individual. The implications of this vision for local government has involved new financial controls, shifts in the balance between markets and state in meeting people's need, organizational reform and changes in the methods of funding local services.

Local authorities have, not unexpectedly, responded in different ways. Conservative-controlled London boroughs, like Wandsworth and Westminster, have used the changes in national climate and legislative provision to pursue distinctive forms of radical Conservatism, as have some shire districts like Derby and Nottingham. On the Left, opposition from Labour-controlled councils has varied in form and extent, from the 'fancy-footwork' of creative accounting, to out-and-out opposition as in the case of Liverpool and Lambeth.

The initiative for reform has not, of course, rested wholly with the radical Right. Indeed, in many ways it was the promotion of radical initiatives by the Left and Centre – including experiments in decentralisation, community politics and 'local socialism' – that preceded and, some would argue, evoked the present reaction by the Right.

There can be no doubt that battle has now been well and truly joined; the evolving 'politicization' of local government (Gyford 1985) has been underpinned by a variety of social changes, and such trends have

1

ushered in a new era for local politics. At the same time the Prime Minister and her government have began to give particular attention to ways of recapturing the older industrial cities from the control of Labour's 'municipal socialists'.

Thatcherism and local government

This book sets out to make sense of the 'Thatcherite' challenge to local government. It is, first and foremost, a contribution to the study of contemporary politics, using 'politics' in the broad and multi-faceted way deployed by Ponton and Gill. They define politics as the way in which 'we understand and order social affairs' especially ' the allocation of resources, the principles underlying this, and the means by which some people or groups acquire and maintain a greater control over the situation than others' (Ponton and Gill 1988). Such a definition suggests that in examining a phenomenon like Thatcherism, and its impact on local government, it is necessary to focus on both theory and practice, ideology and principle , as well as practical policymaking and day-to-day political action. Discussion of the politics of Thatcherism, and of its impact on local government requires, therefore, the deployment of analysis at four inter-linked levels: the politics of ideas and ideology; interest and class politics; the politics of policy; and the politics of statecraft.

The politics of ideas and ideology

Thatcherism has been identified with particular ideas, values and doctrines – sound money, free markets, individual freedom, stable family life and traditional morality, to name but a few. Indeed such ideas have been put forward so explicitly, and argued for so insistently that some commentators have suggested that Thatcherism represents a new form of Conservatism, one that is guided by principles and 'driven' by ideas, and is altogether less pragmatic and opportunistic than earlier Tory traditions. For others, the more interesting (albeit linked) feature of Conservative politics in the late twentieth century is the way in which the Conservative party leadership have made efforts to take and retain the initiative in the battle for ideas. This is witnessed in the growth of various backroom policy centres and think tanks, and the deployment of skilled media consultants and public relations professionals to promote the Conservative message in clear and electorally acceptable ways. Such developments have certainly had their impact on local government. Radical ideas for new policy machinery have been developed, and then translated into action; urban development corporations, grant-aided schools, Housing Action Trusts and other examples of creative policy development will be discussed in the chapters that follow. The more general attempt to take the initiative in replacing post-war 'Butskellism' with a new Right-of-Centre consensus has created a fertile ground for the promotion of new political agendas and practical reform programmes.

Interest and class politics

The definition of politics utilized above emphasized the importance of the way in which people and groups organize to acquire and maintain control over the allocation of scarce resources. A study like this must, therefore, be concerned with the ways in which policy change serves to reinforce, or undermine, the interests of particular groups and classes in society. Without minimizing the importance of political ideas as guides to political action, it is also vital to examine the material and social interests served by specific policy changes (like the introduction of the community charge) as well as the long-term outcomes of attempts to modify social and political assumptions (e.g. about the proper balance between local markets and local government in meeting people's need for housing).

The politics of policy

Both ideas and interests are deployed in shaping and justifying policy development and implementation. Since 1979 three successive Conservative administrations have been extremely active in promulgating and executing a great range of policies which, directly or indirectly, affect the operation, and in many respects the very *raison d'etre*, of local government in Britain. Webb and Wistow (1982) have provided a categorization of types of public policy and we can adapt their contribution with profit to help identify the major strands of policy development that will pre-occupy us in this book:

(a) Resource policies: these relate to desired levels and mixes of financial, manpower and capital resources for deployment (in our case) within local government, as well as policies concerning the most appropriate methods of raising revenues to support such expenditure.

(b) Service policies: these define appropriate mixes and methods of meeting need in different service areas, provide guidance for the determination of priorities between different client groups, and · specify the 'output' criteria to be used in evaluating the success or otherwise of the services offered.

(c) Governance policies: these relate to definitions of the proper role of government (central and local), the structuring of relations between government 'tiers' and between governmental and non-governmental bodies.

Ensuing chapters examine a wide range of recent initiatives under each of these headings: the community charge, cash limits, rate capping and competitive tendering, etc. (resource policies); council house sales, open school rolls, urban development corporations, etc. (service policies); and increased central controls and the use of MSC (the Training Commission) and other quangos as policy instruments (Governance policies).

The politics of statecraft

Government policy cannot be implemented, interests served, and principles realized unless an administration is able to mobilize political support and ward off opposition in electoral and party-political terms. Statecraft (following Bulpitt 1985) refers to political action orientated to the pursuit of office, the management of power, and the organization of the party machine for electoral success. A common theme in many chapters in this book concerns the evolving nature of Thatcherite statecraft. This is examined most significantly with reference to central government's attempts to manage and influence the actions of democratic and autonomous local government in Britain, and in overcoming and containing those strategies adopted by some local councils to preserve or maximize their own policy autonomy.

A guide to the book

This book has been prepared so that it can be read either as a whole, or approached as a series of topics to be 'dipped-into', in line with the reader's particular interests. We assume that the reader will have a basic familiarity with the structure and functions of local government, and also own to some knowledge about the political predispositions and policy thrusts of the three Conservative administrations led by Margaret Thatcher since 1979 (the following provide useful background in this respect: Elcock 1982; Parkinson 1987; Drucker *et al.* 1986; Hampton 1987; and Stoker 1988).

Chapter 2 does, nevertheless, provide an historical background to the development of local government and local politics in Britain. It suggests that the tradition of multi-functional local government was, historically, supportive to the development of local democracy and local policy autonomy. In so far as the Thatcherite challenge to local government has encouraged the development of appointed, single purpose agencies and authorities so its impact has been towards the weakening of local choice and the containment of local variability in policy and provision.

Chapter 3 continues the historical theme and seeks to locate the Thatcherite project for local government in terms of contested views about the nature of modern Conservatism. For many commentators Thatcherism is seen to represent a break with traditional Tory thought and doctrine. The argument here is that there has been an attempt to break with Conservative visions of post-war social democracy (and its 'Municipal Toryism' equivalent in local government) but that the Thatcherite project of the 1980s and 1990s is better seen as an attempt to reassert, and return to, an older and deeper-rooted Conservative tradition.

Chapter 4 turns from ideas and ideology to policy, specifically to central government's resource policies and the concerted bid that Mrs Thatcher's administrations have made to gain control over the 'local authority' element of public expenditure. This analysis further demonstrates that local government is losing its scope and autonomy to innovate policy in response to local need.

Chapter 5 deepens the exploration of the general themes introduced in the first three chapters, through a discussion of the impact of Thatcherism on local public service provision. Taking housing, education and personal social services as exemplars of the thrust of recent policy changes it concludes that apparent ambiguities and contradictions in policy (e.g. centralization of the school curriculum – and educational decentralization, by allowing schools to opt for grant-aided status) are dissolved if ideological and resource explanations are augmented with interest-group explanations.

Chapters 6 and 7 explore developments in two further policy arenas in which local government has traditionally played a promotional role. Chapter 6 examines the recent history of initiatives in local economic development. The picture that emerges is one of uneven and patchy policy initiation and implementation, with urban left authorities in particular finding it increasingly difficult to stimulate local economic regeneration in an era of public expenditure constraint. This chapter provides further analysis of centralization in policy development and of the willingness of central government to 'by-pass' established local government, this time via the device of the new urban development corporations. Chapter 7 examines the role played by local government in reinforcing and reproducing racial inequality. The impact of Thatcherism on struggles for racial equality is addressed, and the question posed how far has the impact of Thatcherism been one of reinforcing popular racism, and marginalizing the anti-discriminatory programmes of local government?

Chapter 8 turns from an examination of the politics of policy, ideology, and statecraft within particular policy arenas to an assessment of their cumulative effect on the governance of local authorities in Britain. Contemporary efforts to move beyond the 'bureaucratic-paternalism' of the post-war years are examined in terms of a number of reform tendencies that, it is suggested, can be boiled down to one fundamental issue: should the reform of local authority governance be focused on achieving greater accountability to the elector and taxpayer, or is there still room for a more collectivist approach to broad-based social and economic development by local government?

In the final chapter we summarize and synthesize the arguments and conclusions of the preceding chapters. We suggest that the Thatcherite challenge to local government embraces two, related, missions. First, a bid to recast the local socio-political order, and second, an attempt to refashion the nature of the local political process. These two over-arching themes lead us to identify three possible versions of the 'model authority' of the 1990s. We call them the 'contract authority', the 'enterprising authority' and the 'business-corporatist authority'. Each represents an effort, on the part of Conservative administrations, to come to terms with the 'challenge of Thatcherism' in the context of the socio-political realities of their own localities.

References

Bulpitt, J. (1985) 'The Discipline of the new democracy: Mrs Thatcher's domestic statecraft' in *Political Studies* xxxiv (1).

Drucker, H., Dunleavy, P., Gamble, A., and Peele, G. (eds) (1986) *Developments in British Politics 2*, Basingstoke: Macmillan.

Elcock, H. (1982) *Local Government*, London: Methuen.

Gyford, J. (1985) 'The Politicisation of Local Government' in M. Loughlin, M. D. Gelfand, and K. Young (eds) *Half a Century of Municipal Decline 1935–1985*, London: Allen & Unwin.

Hampton, W. (1987) *Local Government and Urban Politics*, London: Longmans.

Parkinson, M. (ed.) (1987) *Reshaping Local Government*, Hermitage: Policy Journals.

Ponton, G. and Gill, P.(1988) *Introduction to Politics*, Second Edition, Oxford: Basil Blackwell.

Stoker, G. (1988) *The Politics of Local Government*, Basingstoke: Macmillan.

Webb, A. and Wistow, G. (1982) *Whither State Welfare?*, London: Royal Institute of Public Administration.

Chapter two

Local government in historical perspective

Introduction

Local government has rarely if ever been more controversial, and local politics has never aroused so much interest. For years local government has been regarded as essentially worthy, but dull. Its role was largely taken for granted, for although little systematic thought was given to the range of functions which should be given to democratic local government, there was a broad consensus that elected local authorities were very largely doing the right kind of things. Party manifestoes issued at general elections made brief ritual tributes to the value of local government, but it was not regarded as the stuff of political conflict, even when apparently far-reaching changes to its structure or management were on the agenda. The media paid scant attention to local politics, and few if any local politicians rose to national prominence in the post-Second World War era, at least until the late 1970s.

All that has changed. Local government is now news. Some local politicians are better known and more readily recognized than many cabinet ministers. Local government was a central issue in the 1987 general election, and a series of controversial bills affecting the future of local government have clogged Parliament's legislative programme. Polarization and sharp ideological conflict have increasingly characterized the local political arena, which has become the testing ground for experiments in local socialism and municipal Thatcherism.

Partly as a consequence, the values and processes of local government itself, long taken for granted, have increasingly been called into question. Local government in the United Kingdom is now in the process of a radical and quite fundamental transformation. The changes taking place under the auspices of the Thatcher Government reflect more than a shift in administrative fashion. They involve a radically new conception of local government, with, potentially at least, a sharply reduced role for elected politicians, and indeed local politics as it has been practised previously. The future shape of local government is not

7

yet entirely clear, and will not be until the full implications of a number of trends now in process are finally worked out. Some of these trends may yet be reversed, but it seems probable that local government in the twenty-first century will be qualitatively different from the local government of the last hundred years. Local authorities may cease to be the main providers of services. Instead they will assume a regulatory role, with perhaps only a residual involvement in the direct provision of services. Expenditure and employment may contract sharply. The scope for effective choice through local representative institutions will be limited.

The far reaching changes now taking place can only be understood against the background of the history and development of the local government system in the UK over the last one hundred and fifty or so years. Only with a thorough understanding of the essence of UK local government and politics, as it has been traditionally practised is it possible to appreciate the full extent of the revolution currently in progress.

Local services and the limits of state action

One very obvious feature of UK local government is the very wide range of services and functions for which it has been responsible. Moreover, while some of these functions involve a regulatory role, most have involved direct service provision. Many central government departments have had little responsibility for the direct provision of services, and have performed an essentially supervisory, promotional, or regulatory role. Local authorities, by contrast, have been intimately involved with the day-to-day running of services. How did local government acquire such wide-ranging responsibilities? While a few functions had existed for centuries, the vast bulk of modern local government services were the product of the nineteenth and twentieth centuries (Smellie 1968; Redlich and Hirst 1970). Substantially they were the consequence of industrialization, and the rapid expansion and concentration of population associated with it. Urban living on this scale was essentially a new phenomenon, and created new needs for government intervention, and posed old problems in a far more acute form.

Among these old problems were law and order, and poverty, but both required a fundamentally new approach. It was no accident that the creation of a modern police force was the product of the nineteenth century. The growth of cities presented new opportunities for crime, and the disintegration of traditional communities removed some constraints on antisocial behaviour. The need to protect the new prosperity of the industrial bourgeoisie from the feared underclasses inhabiting the slums of the major industrial cities, was a major incentive to spend public money on police and prisons. Even some projects of civic improvement, seemingly unrelated to law and order, were partly inspired by a need to deter crime. Street lighting was more than a pleasant civic amenity – it was a deterrent to acts of robbery and violence which would otherwise have been concealed under cover of darkness.

Poverty also was an old problem posed in a more acute and dangerous form. The escalating burden of the poor rate, coupled with potentially dangerous concentrations of the poor and unemployed in cities were major factors in the New Poor Law of 1834. This, based on free market principles, and designed to reduce levels of state support and expenditure, paradoxically created a vast new bureaucracy, to administer a service which continued to grow in size and scope (Fraser 1984).

Public health, by contrast, was an essentially new preoccupation. Fear of contagious diseases which threatened middle-class suburbia, as well as the urban poor, fuelled a virtual crusade for public intervention to secure a pure water supply, provide sewers, and control noxious trades (Fraser 1976, 1984).

It is a point worth emphasizing that the initial growth of services was not the product of some new-found enthusiasm for collectivist solutions, as is sometimes suggested by present-day New Right critics. Some post hoc rationalization of the massive expansion of government intervention which took place in the nineteenth century was subsequently supplied by New Liberals and Fabian Socialists, but the initial developments took place despite the dominant free-market ideology, and despite strong pressures from ratepayers for retrenchment. It was the failure of private enterprise to supply pure water, drains and sewers, and control the lethal by-products of its own manufacturing activities which persuaded a former enthusiast for free market solutions such as Edwin Chadwick to embrace state intervention (Finer 1952).

Similarly, direct state provision was usually the last rather than the first resort, as is clearly shown in education. The initial response was for the government to supply some limited financial assistance to voluntary bodies. It was only the failure of the voluntary system to provide schools on the scale and quality required that eventually forced a reluctant government to 'fill in the gaps'. This was a pattern repeated with other services. Only after exhortation, regulation, and financial aid to voluntary organizations had all failed to produce the desired results was direct public provision generally accepted.

Of course, new public services, once established, created their own vested interests of public service professionals, workers and consumers. Bureaucratic and electoral pressures doubtless help to explain the rapid expansion of some of these services. Yet the parallel development of

9

similar services in virtually every other advanced industrial nation provides some *prima facie* evidence that the growth in state services and expenditure which took place was the corollary of the process of industrialization itself, rather than some wilful indulgence in a mania for collectivist solutions. Only perhaps the scale of public housing in the United Kingdom might be regarded as at all untypical against the experience of the growth of public intervention in other countries.

What perhaps does require some further explanation is why these public services became the prime responsibility of local rather than national agencies. Local administration of a kind was clearly necessary, but services might have been provided by specialist local agencies under close bureaucratic supervision from the centre.

Some developments were essentially the consequence of local initiatives. General legislation, as in the case of public health, often followed Private Acts secured by local authorities (Fraser 1984). This was a pattern which was to be repeated again and again in social policy. Local experiments pioneered by individual local authorities have often led ultimately to the establishment of a new national policy.

One explanation for reliance on local provision was the relative absence of appropriate administrative machinery at national level. Neither the bureaucracy, nor even embryo departments, existed to assume vast new supervisory responsibilities. Admittedly, little more existed at local level, but at least there were authorities and agencies already in being which could be adapted or reformed to assume the new roles required. Ancient administrative bodies such as the counties and boroughs, and even the parishes, could be utilized, in parallel with mushrooming special purpose authorities. In general. though, the adaptation of old institutions rather than the development of wholly new ones has been favoured in the United Kingdom, where a reverence for tradition and an attachment to a gradualist, incrementalist approach is rooted in mainstream political thought and culture.

There was additionally some ideological prejudice against centralist solutions. Partly this was a legacy of the successful revolt of the Whig aristocrats and traders against the centralizing tendencies of the Stuarts. It also reflected antiquarian myths about self-governing Anglo-Saxon localities (Anderson 1967). Yet the strength of the anti-centralist convictions of such as Toulmin Smith was real enough, and he only expressed more vehemently than most a pervasive element of Victorian political culture. Even Disraeli, often seen as the embodiment of paternalist interventionist Conservatism had, according to his biographer, Blake, 'a genuine hatred of centralization, bureaucracy, and every manifestation of the Benthamite state' (Blake 1966).

In the nineteenth century there was also no technological imperative for national organization or even supra-local organization, as far as most services were concerned. A city, or even a medium-sized town, could comfortably handle its own water, gas, and subsequently electricity supply. Law and order was still essentially a local concern. State involvement with education was largely a matter of providing elementary schools, a task within the scope of comparatively small local authorities.

So local authorities rapidly accumulated a wide range of functions, some statutory, some permissive, some regulatory, and some administrative. Little serious thought was given to the kind of functions which a local authority might reasonably exercise. Instead responsibilities grew almost haphazardly. The growth of local government services was in some senses the natural corollary of a general growth of collectivist tendencies in the nineteenth and twentieth centuries. Yet there was also a developing tension between national and local provision. Both world wars involved a significant expansion of collectivism, but within the public sector a marked centralization. Local government thus gained responsibilities from the general expansion of state intervention, but lost control of some services to the centre. The losses, although significant enough, were largely masked by the development of new services and the continued expansion of old ones. Thus until the late 1970s, the history of local government seemed to involve a steady, almost relentless, expansion of services, employment and expenditure.

It is important to recall that until comparatively recently, while there was plenty of criticism of the structure, finance and internal management of local government, there was virtually no criticism of the extent of its responsibilities. Reports simply assumed that the existing range of services would continue to be provided. The issue was how far and how fast services and expenditure should be allowed to grow, not whether they should be direct local government responsibilities at all. The loss of services which did occur – substantially the public utilities, trunk roads, health and water – was not, by and large, attributable to any ideological hostility to local government. Rather they were publicly regretted exceptions to the general presumption in favour of local authority control, and justified in terms of special technological or administrative circumstances.

Local government was thus largely unprepared to face the fundamental challenge to its whole traditional range of functions and administrative responsibilities which has been such a marked feature of the Thatcher Government. The reasons for local government provision of education, housing, social services, recreational facilities, waste collection and disposal had been taken for granted so long, as scarcely to need defending. Important debates did take place on the internal organization of major services, but not over local government's continued responsibility for them. Recent years have thus seen a qualitative shift in the whole character of the debate over these services, which is no longer over how local authorities should exercise their responsibilities for these services, but whether they should still be direct local government responsibilities at all.

Local elections, politics and power

The sheer range and extent of service provision, employment and expenditure is clearly a crucial aspect of UK local government, although many would not regard this as its most critical feature, but rather its democratic character. Local government involves elected local authorities. Democracy is often seen as a key, almost defining characteristic of English local government. On the other hand the practice, and more recently even the principle, of local democracy has attracted considerable criticism. The by-passing of local government which has been such a marked feature of recent years would not have been allowed to happen had the health and vitality of local democratic institutions been generally admitted. The democratic character of local government is a central but contentious issue (Young 1986; Stoker 1988).

Sometimes it is regretted that local government should involve party politics, or even any form of politics. This is a rather naïve view. Decisions over service levels or policy do not involve purely technical considerations, to be determined by professionally-qualified experts. They involve gains and losses for individuals, groups, and sometimes whole communities. A wide range of interests are involved – taxpayers, service users, service providers, sectional pressure groups and political parties. Much that is written on local government still implies a dispassionate search for administrative rationality. But people gain and lose from local government services, and from proposed changes in the range and type of provision. Living standards and the whole quality of life may be affected by a decision to change a bus route, close a school, increase the provision of home helps, raise council house rents or cut the subsidy on recreational facilities. Behind abstruse debates lies the endless political struggle over who gets what. Local government thus inescapably involves politics.

The intensity of partisan conflict in local government has become more marked in recent years, perhaps for the obvious reason that more is at stake, but such conflict is by no means new. It was a feature of Victorian city government (Hennock 1973; Fraser 1976, 1979; Garrard 1983). Conflict over office and the fruits of office, over services and expenditure, over the whole form and direction of municipal government was always manifest, and often ferocious. The 1835

Municipal Corporations Act, which in some senses laid the foundations for the development of our modern local government system was bitterly attacked by Tories nationally and locally, who regarded it not just as a partisan Whig measure but as an act of expropriation depriving members of existing corporations of their legitimate rights, privileges and property. The Nonconformist Whig businessmen who frequently took control of the leading Victorian cities after 1835 enjoyed the status and power they had previously been denied by their Tory rivals. But local politics involved more than contests for office and the fruits of office. Often they divided whole communities. Conflicts within and between social groups were sometimes complicated by sectarian religious rivalries and other divisions. Ideological conflict between civic improvers and enthusiasts for the 'municipal gospel' on the one hand, and 'retrenchers' or 'economists' on the other, rivalled in intensity modern conflicts between the new urban Left and Municipal Thatcherists. Local elections were thus of vital importance to those groups contending directly for power, and of considerable significance to the bulk of the community initially excluded from direct participation.

The elective principle was widely adopted in the course of the nineteenth century, not only for the reformed traditional authorities, but also for most of the special purpose authorities, such as the poor law unions, local boards of health and subsequently school boards, which mushroomed with the identification of new needs for state action. The trend towards local democratic institutions in the nineteenth century was largely the corollary of parliamentary reform and the extension of the national franchise. Thus the first Great Reform Bill of 1832 which reformed and marginally extended the parliamentary franchise, paved the way for the 1835 Municipal Corporations Act. The 1888 and 1894 Local Government Acts which established a national system of elected local authorities followed the 1867 and 1884 Reform Acts. The gradual and in some quarters grudging acceptance of the principle of parliamentary democracy had rendered increasingly anomalous and unacceptable the continued administration of the counties by unelected Justices of the Peace (Smellie 1968; Redlich and Hirst 1970).

Thus the local franchise grew roughly in parallel with the parliamentary franchise. The initial developments did not depend on any theory of local democracy. It was left to later theorists to argue that local democratic institutions were as important, perhaps even more important, than national democratic institutions. De Tocqueville's writings, and his championship of free local institutions as the basis of liberty, received a more ready acceptance in the English speaking world than in his native France. Romantic antiquarians like Toulmin Smith strove for a recovery of ancient local liberties which were largely imaginary, but still potent as myths. John Stuart Mill hoped that local democratic institutions would provide an education in democracy, and that local councils would furnish 'nurseries of statesmen'(Hill 1974).

Significantly perhaps, although democratic theory in general has been subject to substantial modifications, refinements, and alternative formulations since the nineteenth century, the theory of local democracy has scarcely advanced beyond the arguments set out by Mill and other Victorians. Marx, the classical elitists, Weber, and the pluralists have all had a profound influence on democratic theory. At a more practical level, the degeneration of parliamentary democracies into fascist or military dictatorships, coupled with the more prosaic work of social scientists on voting and other aspects of the democratic process, has eroded the easy optimism of nineteenth-century democrats. Yet the justifications for local democratic institutions have remained as it were pickled in aspic, just as they were left by Mill and de Tocqueville. Support for local democracy has become what Mill would have described as a dead dogma, an article of faith, enfeebled by the lack of real challenge, sustained only by long usage, and upheld without understanding.

The practice of local democracy has perhaps left something to be desired. Turnout in local elections has been persistently low. Surveys have revealed widespread ignorance of the functions, personnel, and processes of local government. Analysis of local voting behaviour suggests that local elections are determined essentially by national trends (Sharpe 1967; Newton 1976; Dunleavy 1980; and Miller's research for Widdicombe Cmnd 9800, HMSO). All this somewhat weakens the idea of councils fully accountable to their local communities. Right wing critics of local government have further argued that accountability is also blurred by the relatively weak link between local taxation and local expenditure. Only a minority of electors pay rates in full, while only around a quarter of local government expenditure is financed by domestic rates anyway. Profligate councillors are thus able to indulge in high cost schemes, without those who elect them having to bear the price (Walker 1983). Radical critics by contrast have criticized local government for being remote, bureaucratic and insensitive, and failing to encourage more direct citizen involvement and participation (Cockburn 1977; Boddy and Fudge 1984; Hoggett and Hambleton 1987).

Some of this criticism may be exaggerated, and some may equally apply to the exercise of democracy at the parliamentary level, but it has to be conceded that local democracy in practice falls somewhat short of the ideal. Local government has scarcely provided an education in democracy, as Mill hoped. On the other hand there are still a number of points that can be made about elected local authorities, even in their

14

present imperfect form. They do ensure a degree of responsiveness by decision-makers to the local community. Local government, remote and insensitive though it may be, is considerably more open than most of the rest of the public sector. Rather more people do have a chance of participating in key decisions which affect them, even if that participation is effectively restricted. Elected councillors may be far from typical of those they represent, but they are far more socially representative than the members of appointed authorities. Without local government, political parties would have nothing to exist for at local level, and would become even more centralized, bureaucratic and unresponsive than they are at the moment. Power would become even more centralized.

If elected local authorities were as useless as some of their critics have alleged, there would be little point in bothering to weaken or destroy them. It is because they do provide some kind of check on the far-reaching plans of the Thatcher Government to transform the whole character of Britain's political economy, culture and society, and because their elective character gives them a degree of legitimacy in asserting and maintaining an alternative approach to public intervention, that the government has taken them on.

Local agencies and communities

An aspect of local government which has so far only been alluded to obliquely in passing is its multi-purpose nature. In the nineteenth century, multi-purpose local authorities co-existed with a number of special purpose agencies. The initial response to the revelation of some new need for public intervention was to create a special purpose body to handle the function. Thus turnpike trusts were established to build roads, improvement commissions to provide street lighting and paving, poor law unions to administer the new poor law, school boards to build and staff schools, and local boards of heath to undertake responsibilities established by the expanding public health legislation.

This development of new agencies was not the consequence of any consciously articulated administrative theory. In part the new agencies were a reflection on the relative unsuitability of the unreformed traditional authorities. Nor did the special purpose agencies really involve any radical departures of principle. Even the poor law unions, the most radical and the most criticized of the administrative innovations, did not involve wholly new administrative areas on the revolutionary French pattern, but unions of parishes. Moreover, as has already been noted, they were commonly elected, albeit with fancy weighted franchises where the number of votes was related to the ownership of property. Their constitution thus reflected the same

15

Victorian faith in representative institutions which was leading to the reform and reconstitution of more traditional authorities. There was little conscious attempt to weigh the respective merits of single-purpose and multi-purpose authorities. They grew haphazardly alongside each other, in response to the rapid expansion of perceived needs.

It was practical rather than theoretical considerations which eventually led to a rationalization of the whole system of local administration, and the victory of the multi-purpose principle. The proliferation of authorities was seen to lead to duplication, waste, conflict and confusion. The unreformed system of local government prior to 1888 was neatly characterized by the Liberal Unionist politician, Goschen, as 'a chaos as regards authorities, a chaos as regards rates, and a worse chaos than all as regards areas'. His solution was a comprehensive system of multi-purpose authorities responsible for all local services. This was largely achieved by the Acts of 1888 and 1894. Education was subsequently brought within the system of elected multi-purpose authorities in 1902, and the administration of poor relief was briefly transferred to local government in 1929.

Multi-purpose authorities fitted comfortably with the notion of local democratic institutions. Elected single-purpose authorities are not unthinkable. Most of the ad hoc bodies created in the nineteenth century were elected. Elected school boards are widespread in the United States, and similar elected single-purpose bodies are occasionally found in other countries. Moreover there has been a recent, although scarcely auspicious UK example, the short-lived Inner London Education Authority. It is not difficult to understand, however, why such elected single-purpose authorities are not found more often. Their proliferation would lead in all probability to greater public confusion and apathy. Inevitably they would involve some curtailment of local choice, as the determination of priorities would be confined to within rather than between services. Here, the advice of the expert, the qualified professional, would almost certainly predominate, reducing the role of the elected layman to one of public watchdog only. Professional dominance, always a strong possibility, is much more likely in single service authorities, where there is often a single dominant profession. In a multi-purpose authority the elected representative can to an extent balance the competing claims of rival professions and services, and there is more scope for the local determination of priorities (Leach 1986).

This implies in turn a focus on the needs of particular communities rather than particular services. A service focus tends to involve national priorities determined by professionals with strong loyalties to their national professional associations. In such a context, local administrative areas are determined by the technical requirements of the service rather than any objective or subjective idea of community. A multi-purpose authority, by contrast, suggests a local community with some common interests, and needs which the community itself can best determine. Notions of community and social geography have indeed been employed to assist in the determination of local government administrative areas in partial and comprehensive reorganizations (Cmnd 4040, HMSO 1969).

Admittedly this community focus has hardly in practice been one of the more conspicuous features of UK local government. Indeed some cynics would suggest that community has been consistently sacrificed to service requirements and notions of economic rationality in local government reorganizations. Local authorities such as Tameside or Kirklees scarcely correspond to any sense of community or shared interests. Moreover, the proliferation of professions, departments, and specialist service committees has led in practice to fragmentation and a service mentality. Yet despite all this, the multi-purpose framework has always afforded a potential counterweight to specialism and professionalism. The point was put eloquently by the Bains Committee.

> Local government is not, in our view, limited to the narrow
> provision of services to the local community...It has within its
> purview the overall economic, cultural, and physical well-being of
> that community.
>
> (Bains 1972: para 2.12)

This is a large claim for local government. It implies that the local authority has the right, indeed duty, to determine community interests, preferences and needs: that local communities, like nations, are not pure fictions. It implies a case for differentiation between communities, for treating the citizens of Walsall differently, in some instances at least, from the citizens of Leeds or Southwark. It implies indeed a justification for diversity and local choice. It suggests at least some limitation on the imposition of uniform, nationally-imposed requirements. The idea of local communities with some distinctive local needs and preferences, and a degree of effective local choice, inescapably implies a degree of local autonomy and some restriction on central control (Jones and Stewart 1983).

The local state and the national state

This leads to the question of central–local relations. It is frequently observed that local government has no special constitutional status in the United Kingdom. UK local government has always had to operate within the parameters of a unitary state. Parliament is sovereign. The system of elected local authorities which evolved in the nineteenth century was established by Acts of Parliament. The structure, functions, finance, and even the very existence of local government can be altered by a simple majority at Westminster. Local authorities themselves can do nothing without statutory authority. They have no general capacity to act in the interests of their local communities. They are bound by the 'ultra vires' principle (Buxton 1973).

But the distribution of power and the operation of the policy-making process in practice is not determined by abstract constitutional principles. For a long time the notion of parliamentary sovereignty was also rather less restrictive than it might appear. In the early and mid-nineteenth century cabinet dominance of the legislative process was less marked. Then much legislation was private rather than public, a large part pushed through by local authorities desirous of acquiring specific powers within their own areas. Nor were public bills, then overwhelmingly government bills, as they are today. Moreover, some public bills were modelled on earlier private bills initiated by local authorities themselves. Much legislation was permissive rather than mandatory, and gave councils considerable discretion over implementation.

Even later, when the government came to dominate Parliament's legislative programme the sweeping powers apparently given to ministers were more apparent than real. The more draconian were seldom or never used. General powers to determine and implement national policy in the preambles of acts were not backed up by detailed specific powers to make such sweeping responsibilities a reality. Crucially, ministers and central government departments lacked the resources for effective control of services. The Department of Education and Science for example did not directly employ a single teacher or run a single school. With a headquarters staff of around a thousand, it lacked the capacity to run education. In such circumstances national initiatives were heavily dependent on local cooperation.

But an additional reason why local authorities enjoyed considerable autonomy in practice was that there was little real opposition between central and local government for most of the time. Possibly this was because both central government and the vast majority of local authorities then operated within a broad political consensus. There were problems with a few specific local authorities like Poplar which challenged prevailing values, but these were exceptions (Branson 1979). Local government was not generally perceived to be in conflict with national government. An unthinking acceptance of the values and processes of democratic local government was part of a shared political culture. Hostility to centralization, and an attachment to independent local institutions was an aspect of that culture.

In general the centre preferred the carrot to the stick. In these days when the rate support grant seems to be viewed principally as a weapon to restrain or punish over-spending, it is perhaps important to recall that central grants in the nineteenth century were employed to encourage tightfisted local councils to spend more money on particular services. Grants, whether on a unit or percentage basis, were frequently open-ended. Although the extent of local government's financial dependence aroused some concern even in the nineteenth century, it was not then considered to involve a major constraint on local government's freedom of action. The subsequent replacement of specific grants by general grants gave local authorities even more freedom to determine their own priorities (Foster *et al.* 1980).

In general, local government and national government were not seen to be fighting with each other for resources. Before the 1961 Plowden Report there was no attempt to plan and control public expenditure as a whole. Local government finances were a separate matter. Local authorities possessed significant taxing powers in the form of the rates, which gave them a degree of financial independence. Monies raised locally and spent locally were not thought to be a matter for central economic planning.

Perhaps what needs explaining is why there was not more experimentation and diversity. Why did local government make so little use of its freedom? Why were there so few Poplars? Perhaps if there had been, they would have been effectively restrained, as Poplar was (Branson 1979). Thus the autonomy of local government might be said to rest on its not being exercised. Yet it might be noted that there were other pressures towards uniformity than central government control. The growing professionalism of the local government service established national norms and standards. The emergence of a national culture, with a national media, created a climate which was less tolerant of diversity. More centralized national parties, and powerful interest groups operating nationally provided strong political pressures towards common policies.

Crisis and decline

The system of local government which evolved in the UK thus involved elected multi-purpose authorities, directly responsible for the administration of a wide range of responsibilities, enjoying in practice a significant degree of autonomy from central government. These might almost be regarded as defining characteristics of local government. There is of course much administration of public services at local level which is not so organized – local offices of central departments, and appointed local agencies – but these are not conventionally regarded as 'local government'.

In many ways this system of local government seemed secure. Superficially it had prospered, acquiring an ever larger range of responsibilities, employing more people, securing more recognition and status for it professional bodies. Moreover, the values and processes of democratic local institutions were almost universally accepted (Keith-Lucas and Richards 1978).

Yet beneath a largely unexplored consensus on the general value of local government, there were growing anxieties, particularly from the Second World War onwards, about its health and vitality. The present widely-perceived crisis in local government is not as is often suggested or implied, entirely the product of the Thatcher years. One recent text was entitled *Half a Century of Municipal Decline* (Loughlin *et al*. 1985). Another has indicated the immediate post-war period as the critical turning point in the fortunes of local government (Blunkett and Jackson 1987). This is not all post-hoc rationalization. Critics such as William Robson writing in the 1960s suggested that local government was in state of crisis (Robson 1966). Even when the general case for democratic local government was apparently unchallenged, there were, according to such observers at least, serious weaknesses in the system.

The most obvious trend in the post-war years was the erosion of local government functions. The absorption of the Poor Law Unions in 1929 proved the high water mark of elected multi-purpose local authorities in the UK. By this time virtually all local services were in the hands of elected local councils. The gain of social security functions proved particularly short-lived. Then, in the immediate aftermath of war, local government lost, in addition to public assistance, gas and electricity, hospitals, trunk roads, and rating valuation. Robson and others pinned their hopes for a healthier future for local government on a major reorganization of structure. The assumption was that some of the erosion of functions was caused by an out-of-date structure, and the persistence of too many, too small local authorities, involving a loss of efficiency. Yet when reorganization finally came, in 1974, it was accompanied by the loss of all the water-related services and the community health services.

Some of these losses may have been inevitable. Technological developments rendered the continued municipal control of electricity and gas supply impractical. More questionably, similar considerations might apply to the water industry. A strong case might also be made for uniformity of provision with a minimum of local discretion in the distribution of cash welfare benefits. That implies close bureaucratic supervision from the centre rather than control by local authorities, whose whole rationale arguably involves a degree of discretion in service delivery. However, the most important single, and perhaps avoidable loss was of the health services. Although technical and financial arguments have been advanced to justify the separation of health from local government, it seems that the real reasons were essentially political and professional.

A significant development has been the apparent return to favour of single-purpose authorities, which are almost inevitably appointed rather than elected. As noted above, the history of local government in the nineteenth and early twentieth centuries involved the steady absorption of *ad hoc* single-purpose bodies into the new system of elected multi-purpose authorities. More recently this trend has been reversed. Both water and health were reorganized in ways which weakened or destroyed previous links with local government and involved the establishment of special purpose authorities. The Manpower Services Commission has taken over some of the former education and training functions of local councils. New town development corporations provided a model for the subsequent urban development corporations which effectively by-pass elected local government.

The apparent return to favour of single-purpose authorities, coupled with the increased use of special administrative arrangements to run local services – joint boards, joint committees and the like – has significantly reduced the proportion of local services administered by directly elected local authorities and has seriously fragmented city government. Once virtually all the major local services in the larger towns and cities were in the hands of the local council. Now these services are distributed between the offices of central government departments or national quasi-government agencies, special purpose authorities, joint boards and, over much of the country two tiers of elected government. City government has thus become a confusing jumble of overlapping and conflicting jurisdictions of the kind condemned by Goschen a century ago. Moreover, while the trend may have accelerated in recent years, it began when there still appeared to be a general consensus on the value and importance of local democratic institutions.

The extent of local government's financial dependence on the centre increased significantly in the post-war years. There is no easy formula for determining what proportion of revenue should be derived from local sources to enable local authorities to retain a significant policy-making role. In other countries local government is dependent to varying degrees on the national exchequer. Yet there was widespread concern in the post-war period that local government was becoming over-dependent. By the mid-1970s, grant income was double the yield of rates, both domestic and non-domestic. How far this involved a parallel increase in central control and local autonomy is a moot point. Arguably, the introduction of the general rate support grant, which replaced a number of specific grants in 1956, actually increased the scope for local authorities to determine their own priorities. Yet the increased dependence on central finance did give the government extra leverage over local service provision should they care to use it – and threatened loss of grant has proved a potent weapon of late, in persuading local authorities to cut expenditure.

Increased financial dependence on central government was seen as just one aspect of a general trend towards more central control of local government. Mainstream textbooks of the 1960s and 1970s gloomily catalogued the apparent formidable statutory, administrative, financial and judicial controls over local authorities (Redcliffe-Maud and Wood 1974; Richards 1980). In retrospect this view seems exaggerated. Some of the controls were little used while others were not particularly restrictive. Yet they contributed to a growing concern about the health and vitality of local government.

A major concern was the promotion of greater efficiency. It was widely reckoned that neither the structure of the local government system, nor internal management processes were conducive to efficient operation. Larger units would enable local authorities to reap economies of scale and introduce modern management methods. The calibre of councillors was also held to be deficient – too few businessmen and other suitably qualified people were tempted to enter the council chamber, although actually businessmen were considerably over-represented in terms of their numbers in the general population (Dearlove 1979). If better councillors could not be recruited, the answer was felt by some to be greater delegation to officers, who were increasingly perceived as the real decison-makers anyway (Buxton 1973). Some reformers looked to the American example of professional city managers. The Maud Report (1967) drew on private sector practices to recommend a small management board of leading council members to which officers would be responsible, with other council committees stripped of their executive powers. All this implied an implicit, sometimes explicit downgrading of the democratic and political elements in local government (Dearlove 1979).

The failure of reform

These pressures led to the major reorganization of the structure of local government in 1974, and the accompanying changes in internal organization and processes. Together these seemed to involve a massive transformation of local government as it had been traditionally understood. In retrospect the scale of change, although real enough to those most directly affected, was exaggerated. The local government map was indeed substantially altered. Committee and department structures were modified. There were some changes in the relative status and influence of local government professions – not all of which were sustained. A new terminology and some new techniques were employed. Yet the essence of the old local government system remained intact, somewhat enfeebled (as will be argued later). Local authorities covered wider areas and served more people, but continued to administer the same kinds of services in much the same kind of way (Wood 1976; Alexander 1982).

Moreover, major questions were ducked. There was no attempt to reformulate a theory of democratic local government, no attempt to re-examine the kind of functions which elected local authorities might be expected to operate, no attempt to clarify the relations between central and local government, and determine their relative spheres of operation. The finance of local government was ignored, and the issue of regional government shelved. Some lip service was paid to the need for greater public participation, but most of the changes which took place were in the opposite direction (Cockburn 1977; Hambleton 1979; Boaden *et al.* 1982).

With the wisdom of hindsight it is now fairly clear that the upheavals of the early 1970s largely involved the wrong answers to the wrong questions. The preoccupation of official reports and academics was with the need to reconcile democracy with efficiency. While the paramount importance of democracy was regularly proclaimed it was substantially taken for granted. The major concern was to increase efficiency. This was taken to require larger administrative units, (Cmnd 4040, HMSO 1969) and the importation of business methods (Maud 1967; Dearlove 1979).

It is now evident that the 1974 reorganization has been a failure – an unsatisfactory compromise which in the end has pleased no one. Almost any of the various other approaches to reform might have proved more durable. Perhaps Crossman was initially too impatient with the slow incremental revisions of the Boundary Commission in his determination to go instead for a comprehensive reorganization. Once the need for radical reform was embraced, either the unitary system of all-purpose authorities recommended by the majority report of the Redcliffe-Maud Royal Commission (Cmnd 4040, HMSO, vol. 1 1969), or conceivably the well-argued minority report of Derek Senior with its two-tier system (Cmnd 4040, vol. 2), might have provided a principled foundation for a new structure. The 1972 Act by contrast involved an awkward combination of fashionable ideas and political expediency (Wood 1976; Alexander 1982).

Thus the Conservatives took on board the need for larger administrative units, despite the failure of research commissioned by Redcliffe-Maud to demonstrate any clear link between size and efficiency. They also adopted what was perhaps the most questionable aspect of the commission's proposals – for a special two-tier system in the major conurbations – while rejecting the general case for unitary authorities elsewhere. Even so, they crippled the new metropolitan counties at birth by reducing their boundaries and functions (Leach 1985). Elsewhere in England the Conservatives went for a modified two-tier system based on the old shire counties, which reflected their own party strength and interests rather than any coherent administrative rationale (Wood 1976; Alexander 1982). This should not be a matter for surprise. Politics is about power, and the boundaries of local authorities affect, sometimes critically, the chances of winning power locally. Thus while public debates over reorganization are likely to be couched in terms of the public interest and administrative rationality, a key influence on the outcome is likely to be party interests and pressures. Even so, neither the 1963 reorganization of London government nor the reorganization of the rest of England and Wales in 1974 can be regarded as particularly effective Tory gerrymanders. In both cases the desire of suburban Conservative Associations to stay out of the cities ran counter to wider Conservative electoral interests. The Tories thus made it more difficult for themselves to win control of the major urban centres.

The reorganization was expected to last at least a generation. Instead the metropolitan counties together with the slightly older Greater London Council(GLC) are already abolished, leaving a local government map more confused and illogical than before. There is no longer any real justification for a different structure in the major conurbations from that in the rest of the country. Now there are persistent rumours that one of the tiers in the shires might be abolished in a further reorganization. In Scotland where the recommendations of the Wheatley Report (Cmnd 4150, HMSO 1969) were largely implemented, a question mark hangs over the future of the regions. No one seems to have much faith in what is left of the existing system surviving much longer.

The managerial revolution which accompanied reorganization has proved more cosmetic than real, although in retrospect much of its thrust was misconceived. Certainly there was some validity in the criticism of narrow departmental and professional attitudes in the pre-Maud and Bains period, although the failings of the old system were rather exaggerated (Eddison 1975; Dearlove 1979). A strengthened political executive could have produced the more corporate approach favoured in both the Maud and Bains reports, but Maud largely ignored party politics, and certainly failed to accommodate the realities of party control, while even the more realistic Bains was infused with a managerial rather than a political approach (Maud 1967; Bains 1972). Although new structures were designed for members as well as officers, the suspicion lingered in the minds of many councillors that corporate management was for the officers rather than themselves. The beefed-up chief executive role coupled with the management team of chief officers seemed to involve a pre-empting of decisions on priorities which were properly the sphere of elected members. There was additionally the implicit assumption that problems could be solved in the interests of whole local communities by the application of the appropriate management techniques. The notion that there are inevitably sharp conflicts of interest within communities which may to a degree be accommodated but scarcely resolved was ignored.

The new management ideas were not only apolitical or even anti-political, they also involved a top-down paternalist philosophy which some would argue has proved positively harmful (Bennington 1975; Cockburn 1977). Despite some attempts to stress the importance of a corporate approach at the service delivery end, the general thrust of the corporate management revolution was to encourage authority-wide, top-down, policy planning. The needs of specific areas, and the case for increased citizen involvement, were subjected to the logic of central determination of priorities. Admittedly one reason for this was the feeling that loyalty and support for the new authorities would be undermined if local particularism was encouraged through a more decentralized approach. Whatever the reasons, the changes in the internal management structures and processes of local authorities in the late 1960s and early 1970s arguably made local government more remote, bureaucratic and paternalist, and less responsive to the needs and preferences of individual citizens and communities. This was despite the vogue for participation which was current in the late 1960s, and bore some official fruit in the 1968 Planning Act and associated Skeffington Report (HMSO 1969), and the Seebohm Report on the Social Services (Cmnd 3703, HMSO 1968).

There were additionally two glaring omissions in all the changes in the 1960s and 1970s. In the first place, the issue of regional government was shelved. Both the majority and minority reports of the Royal Commission (Cmnd 4040, HMSO 1969) recommended structures for regional administration, but the whole issue was shelved in anticipation of the future recommendations from the Kilbrandon Commission on the constitution (Cmnd 5460, HMSO 1973). In practice the introduction of a two-tier system of local government over the whole country by the Conservatives effectively reduced the scope for a regional tier, while the incoming Labour Government in 1974 was too concerned with the urgent political need to assuage Scottish and Welsh nationalism to bother too much about devolution to the English regions. The case for regional government was not so much rejected as ignored, until it was too late to do anything about it (Hogwood and Keating 1982).

Perhaps a more significant omission was the failure to reform local government finance along with boundaries, functions and internal management. Unfortunately, by the time the Layfield Report had attempted to remedy this particular deficiency with recommendations for a reformed rating system coupled with local income tax, it was too late (Cmnd 6453, HMSO 1976). It would be difficult to imagine a more awkward time for a major report to appear advocating a substantial increase in local government's taxing powers. It followed substantial and very unpopular rate rises associated with local government reorganization, and accompanied a national financial crisis, which forced the Labour Government to accept help with stringent conditions from the International Monetary Fund (IMF). The projected administrative costs of local income tax may have been a factor in its rejection, but in the immediate circumstances a reform which would have given local authorities more effective control over their own expenditure (and might have permitted spending increases when the government was looking for cuts), would probably have been rejected anyway.

A decade or more of reports, commissions, and reorganizations thus failed to secure the strengthening of democratic local government which reformers had hoped for. Reorganization was expensive and unpopular, and if durability is any criterion of success, a failure. The management revolution tended to reinforce the image of local councils as remote insensitive bureaucracies. Meanwhile health and water functions were lost, regional government ignored, and financial reform ducked. All this meant that local government was not in the best shape to face the challenge presented by the election of the Thatcher Government in 1979.

Partisanship and polarization

The 1967 Maud and 1972 Bains Reports on internal management structures and processes were both closely associated with the reorganization of boundaries and functions – the Bains Committee was explicitly established to advise the new authorities created by reorganization on appropriate management structures. Yet neither anticipated one of the most significant consequences of reorganization for the internal workings of local government – increased party political involvement in local councils, and greater ideological polarization. Anecdotal evidence in the Maud Report supported what was becoming the new conventional wisdom – that policy initiatives came from officers rather than members. Rather unconvincingly, a new distinction of the respective roles of officers and elected members was attempted, but the whole report effectively downgraded the role of ordinary backbench councillors. Bains was more prepared to accommodate active member involvement in the management process, and showed some awareness of the problems party power might create for officers, but recommended against the adoption of one-party policy committees.

The effective merging of former urban areas with rural areas in the 1974 reorganization led to the introduction of party politics almost everywhere (Gyford 1985a; Widdicombe 1986). Members without party labels, once common in the more rural shires, have become almost an extinct species over much of the country. Partisanship has increased in the council chamber as well as on the hustings. The sharing of patronage on a proportionate basis has almost disappeared. Parties with a majority expect to take effective control of the council, including a majority on all committee, and all the committee chairs and vice-chairs. In the larger authorities, leading members increasingly expect accom- modation in council offices, secretarial and research support. Some are virtually full-time, and effectively paid for their services. Officers brought up under the old dispensation have had considerable difficulty adjusting to the altered reality of power. Within a dozen years of the reorganized system coming into being, the Widdicombe Committee was charting a fundamentally altered local council terrain from that on which Maud and Bains had based their assumptions.

One result of these altered practices has been the end of the political consensus over local government. In part this may be seen as just a reflection of the ideological polarization in politics generally. However the sharpening of the political conflict at local level has produced marked changes in policy as well as swings in party electoral fortunes. The Liberals have used their locally-forged brand of 'community politics' as a springboard for a national revival. Labour has moved away from centralized planning to champion 'local socialism' and Conservatives in authorities such as Wandsworth and Southend have pioneered privatization and other market-based approaches to pave the way for national initiatives (Walker 1983; Gyford 1985a, 1985b; Stoker 1988). In the 1950s and 1960s it was sometimes difficult to characterize distinctive party policy approaches at local level. Now the ideological gulf is perhaps wider than in national politics.

The ending of consensus within local government has also contributed to the ending of the consensus over local government. In the 1960s and 1970s, whatever the deficiencies of local government, these were thought to be essentially remediable. Local government was almost universally regarded as a 'good thing' in principle, if not always in practice. That generally benevolent approach by politicians from across the political spectrum no longer exists. It is not just now this or that particular aspect of local government which is under the microscope, but local government itself.

The challenge of Thatcherism

There is a problem with perspective on any changes which are recent or still in progress. There is a risk of over-dramatizing developments which might in time seem relatively innocuous and insignificant. It must further be admitted that there has been a vociferous local government lobby which has regularly cried 'wolf' over proposed changes in the last half century. In most cases the alarm has proved exaggerated. The prophets of doom have spoiled their case by repetition. In some quarters there is now a complacent assumption that local government can adapt to and survive any proposed reform.

Yet it might be suggested, with due caution, that the changes, recent, on-going and proposed, with which local government has had to cope since 1979 represent cumulatively the most serious threat to its health and vitality which has been posed during its entire history. These are significant claims. It has already been noted that some observers have seen local government as being in decline for half a century, and already in a state of crisis by the 1960s. It is also rightly argued that several of the changes which have taken place since 1979 were essentially developments of trends initiated earlier. Even so, it will be argued here that the changes introduced by the Thatcher administration represent a qualitative shift compared with earlier reforms, and do mark a clear challenge to local government as it has been traditionally understood. Significantly, some writers are already referring back to the pre-1975 period as a 'golden age' for local government (Duncan and Goodwin 1988: 98).

The most significant changes have been made in local government finance, the reform of which was effectively ducked in the 1960s and 1970s. These are discussed at greater length elsewhere in this volume. Here it is sufficient to summarize the more important developments.

First, the reform of the grant system, begun in 1980 and subsequently developed, involves a new principle never before advanced – that central government should determine what each local authority should be spending, and penalize 'overspenders' through the grant system. Previously central government had often tried to influence overall local government spending, but it had been accepted that it was up to individual local councils to determine spending within their own areas, provided that spending was lawful.

Second, rate-capping, announced in 1983 and introduced the following year, took central control over local government finance a crucial stage further. Previously it was accepted that local authorities had total discretion over the level of local taxation. The power to limit the rates of specific authorities which exceed spending targets, coupled with reserve general powers to cap the rates has effectively destroyed that principle.

Both the above developments, although Draconian in impact and damaging to the qualified autonomy of local authorities might have been regarded as essentially short-term expedients, pending some more thorough overhaul of local government finance. There was a legitimate argument, developed earlier by the Layfield Committee (Cmnd 6453, HMSO 1976) that local authorities were insufficiently accountable to their electorate, largely because too small a proportion of local expenditure was met from locally-raised taxation. Layfield had suggested that local government could only exercise significant autonomy if it raised more of its own revenue. Thus local income tax was recommended as a supplement to a reformed rating system to secure local accountability. A government genuinely concerned to promote local accountability might have moved in this direction. Instead the Thatcher Government has moved the other way, replacing domestic rates with a highly regressive poll tax, and transforming business rates into a national tax over which local government has no control. While the ostensible objective was to improve accountability, the real objective, as is clear from the whole tenor of the government's Green Paper (Cmnd 9714, HMSO 1986), was further restraint on local government expenditure. As a result of these changes, local authorities will now raise an even smaller proportion of their own expenditure from local taxation. As a result of this, a relatively small increase in local spending will involve a much larger increase in the community charge (four times as large, from the government's own example in the Green Paper). This heavy deterrent to additional expenditure will, it is confidently predicted, reduce variations in spending, and reduce local choice (Minford 1988). The Green Paper sees local authorities as essentially local administrative agencies responsible for the efficient and cost-effective delivery of a range of specified services, and not, as the Bains Report suggested, elected councils responsible for 'the overall economic, cultural and physical well-being' of the community (Bains 1972).

By comparison changes in structure have been less far-reaching, although significant enough. The Thatcher Government has not generally favoured sweeping and comprehensive changes in administrative structures, preferring instead occasional surgical amputations, such as the abolition of area health authorities, and the scrapping of the civil service department and the central policy review staff. The abolition of the GLC and metropolitan counties, and later the Inner London Education Authority (ILEA), was wholly consistent with this general approach. It has left the system of local government in the major conurbations more confusing and less subject to democratic control (Hillyard and Percy-Smith 1988), but it has also destabilized the whole structure. The logic underpinning two separate local government systems for the larger conurbations and the rest of the country has been destroyed, and the truncated structure is thus anomalous (Leach 1986). Further changes are widely predicted, whatever the party complexion of the government at Westminster.

Perhaps the most important changes for the future of local government, potentially more far-reaching than even the changes in finance, have been over some of its major functions and the way in which these are exercised. There has been some continued erosion of functions to appointed bodies, such as the Manpower Services Commission, and there has also been some deliberate by-passing of local government through the creation of new bodies, such as the urban development corporations. Yet far more significant changes have been introduced into the way services are administered through contracting out and privatization.

As we have seen, local government acquired in the course of the last century and a half extensive responsibility for the direct administration of a wide variety of services. It was because of this direct responsibility for the administration of services that expenditure and employment grew to such a marked extent. Some would argue also that this responsibility for service delivery gave local government considerable leverage over policy and ensured a degree of local autonomy. It is this central role in service delivery which is now threatened.

Local authorities, it is now suggested, may cease to be direct providers of services, and assume instead an enabling role. There is indeed much to be said for experimenting with different methods of provision, as was implied when the idea of the enabling role was first formulated (Jones and Stewart 1983). But ministers have seized on the term as a new buzz-phrase to justify their own proposals. Jones and Stewart have since tartly suggested that what the government has in mind is not the enabling authority, but the disabled authority.

What seems to be involved, in practice, is a dramatic contraction in local government responsibility for administering services. Competitive tendering, pioneered by a few 'Municipal Thatcherite' authorities, and now a legal requirement, has led already to marked reduction in the manual workforce, and has taken some traditional local government services out of direct council control (Ascher 1987). The contracting-out of other council services is planned, and it is suggested that even professional services like law and accounting will not be immune.

Major services have been affected by other legislation. Council housing, already reduced by the 'right to buy' legislation, could be transformed into a residual function by the 'pick a landlord' reforms.

Education, for years the most expensive and prestigious of local authority services, could be turned into little more than a co-ordinating function through the effective transfer of some powers downwards to institutions and rather more powers upwards to the Secretary of State. Even this reduced role could be further attenuated if many schools exercise their new right to opt out of local authority control. Some of these developments are reviewed in more detail later in this volume. Here it will merely be noted that together they amount to the most significant reduction in the direct administrative responsibilities of local government that has ever occurred. A major transformation of the role of local government is involved (Flynn and Walsh 1987; Stoker 1988).

The extensive changes following the election of the Thatcher Government in 1979 have come on top of a number of unresolved problems for local government over the previous decades. The current state of local government might be considered against the features associated with the system described earlier in this chapter.

The qualified autonomy of local government has been effectively reduced not just by the financial changes, but by imposed changes in structure, and legislation reducing discretion on specific services. The return to favour of single-purpose agencies has eroded the central position of the local elected council as the all-purpose or multi-purpose provider of local services. The conception of local authorities as representative bodies, responsible for the overall economic, cultural and physical well-being of local communities has been effectively displaced by a renewed narrow emphasis on their responsibility for particular services. Moreover, this responsibility no longer necessarily involves direct council provision. The scale and scope of local authority activity is being substantially reduced. The elective principle, almost a defining characteristic of British local government, apparently remains intact, but even that has been somewhat curtailed, through the changes to government in the metropolitan areas, the removal of some functions from local authority control, and the by-passing of local government in other spheres. The scope for effective local choice has thus been narrowed.

While not all this has happened since 1979, the most significant developments have followed the election of Mrs Thatcher's Government. Moreover, they seem to be a reflection of an altered and far more hostile climate towards local government. It is thus not too much to claim that Thatcherism has involved a quite fundamental transformation of local government as it has evolved over the last century and a half. Detailed aspects of that transformation, and the reasons for it, will be explored further in subsequent chapters.

References

Alexander, A. (1982) *The Politics of Local Government in the United Kingdom*, London: Longman.
Anderson, O. (1967) *A Liberal State at War*, London: Macmillan.
Ascher, K. (1987) *The Politics of Privatisation*, London: Macmillan.
Bains, M. (Chairman) (1972) *The New Local Authorities: Management and Structure*, London: HMSO.
Bennington, J. (1975) Local Government Becomes Big Business, London: CDP Occasional Paper No. 11.
Blake, R. (1966) *Disraeli*, London: Eyre & Spottiswoode.
Blunkett, D. and Jackson, K. (1987) *Democracy in Crisis*, London: Hogarth.
Boaden, N., Goldsmith, M., Hampton, W., and Stringer, P. (1982) *Public Participation in Local Services*, London: Longman.
Boddy, M. and Fudge, C. (eds) (1984) *Local Socialism*, London: Macmillan.
Branson, N. (1979) *Popularism, 1919–1925*, London: Lawrence & Wishart.
Bulpitt, J. (1967) *Party Politics in English Local Government*, London: Longmans.
Buxton, R. J. (1973) *Local Government*, Harmondsworth: Penguin.
Byrne, T. (1986) *Local Government in Britain*, 4th edn., Harmondsworth: Penguin.
Cockburn, C. (1977) *The Local State*, London: Pluto.
Dearlove, J. (1979) *The Reorganisation of British Local Government*, Cambridge: Cambridge University Press.
Duncan, S. and Goodwin, M. (1988) *The Local State and Uneven Development*, Cambridge: Polity.
Dunleavy, P. (1980) *Urban Political Analysis*, London: Macmillan.
Eddison, T. (1975) *Local Government Management and Corporate Planning*, 2nd edn, Leighton Buzzard: Leonard Hill.
Finer, S. (1952) *Life and Times of Edwin Chadwick*, London: Methuen.
Flynn, N. and Walsh, K. (1987) *Competitive Tendering*, University of Birmingham: Institute of Local Government Studies.
Foster, C., Jackman R., and Perlman, M. (1980) *Local Goverment Finance in a Unitary State*, London: Allen & Unwin.
Fraser, D. (1976) *Urban Politics in Victorian England*, Leicester: Leicester University Press.
Fraser, D. (1979) *Power and Authority in the Victorian City*, Oxford: Blackwell.
Fraser, D. (1984) *The Evolution of the British Welfare State*, 2nd edn., London: Macmillan.
Garrard, J. (1983) *Leadership and Power in Victorian Industrial Towns, 1838–1880*, Manchester: Manchester University Press.
Gyford, J. (1985a) 'The Politicisation of Local Government' in M. Loughlin, M. D. Gelfand, and K. Young (eds), *Half a Century of Municipal Decline*, London: Allen & Unwin.
Gyford, J. (1985b) *The Politics of Local Socialism*, London: Allen & Unwin.
Hambleton, R. (1979) *Policy Planning and Local Government*, London: Hutchinson.

Hampton, W. (1987) *Local Government and Urban Politics*, London: Longman.

Hennock, E. P. (1973) *Fit and Proper Persons: Ideal and Reality in 19th Century Urban Government*, London: Edward Arnold.

Hill, M. (1974) *Democratic Theory and Local Government*, London: Allen & Unwin.

Hillyard, P. and Percy-Smith, J. (1988) *The Coercive State*, London: Fontana, Collins.

HMSO, (1969) *Report of the Royal Commission on Local Government in England, 1966–69 (The Redcliffe-Maud Report)*, 3 vols, Cmnd 4040.

HMSO (1969) *Report of the Royal Commission on Local Government in Scotland (The Wheatley Report)*, 2 vols, Cmnd 4150.

HMSO (1973) *Report of the Royal Commission on the Constitution (The Kilbrandon Report)*, Cmnd 5460.

HMSO (1976) *Local Government Finance, Report of the Committee of Enquiry (The Layfield Report)*, Cmnd 6453.

HMSO (1986) *Green Paper, Paying for Local Government*, Cmnd 9714.

Hoggett, P. and Hambleton, R. (eds) (1987) *Decentralisation and Democracy*, University of Bristol: School for Advanced Urban Studies.

Hogwood, B. and Keating. M. (eds) (1982) *Regional Government in England*, Oxford: Oxford University Press.

Jones, G. W. and Stewart, J. (1983) *The Case for Local Government*, London: Allen & Unwin.

Keith-Lucas, B. and Richards, P. (1978) *A History of Local Government in the Twentieth Century*, London: Allen & Unwin.

Leach, B. (1985) 'The Government of the English Provincial Conurbations', *Local Government Studies*, Jan/Feb.

Leach, B. (1986) 'The Structure of Local Government' in M. Goldsmith (ed.) *Essays in Local Government*, West Yorkshire Metropolitan County Council.

Loughlin, M., Gelfand, M., and Young, K. (1985) *Half a Century of Municipal Decline*, London: Allen & Unwin.

Maud, Sir John (1967) *Committee on the Management of Local Government*, vol. 1 Report, London: HMSO.

Minford, P. (1988) 'What Future for Local Government?', Text of speech to Institute of Economic Affairs Conference, 27 April 1988.

Newton, K. (1976) *Second City Politics*, Oxford: Oxford University Press.

Redcliffe-Maud, Lord, and Wood, B. (1974) *English Local Government Reformed*, Oxford: Oxford University Press.

Redlich, J. and Hirst, F. W. (1970) 'The History of Local Government', in B. Keith-Lucas (ed.) *England*, London: Macmillan.

Richards, P. (1980) *The Reformed Local Government System*, London: Allen & Unwin.

Robson, W. (1966) *Local Government in Crisis*, London: Allen & Unwin.

Seebohm, F. (Chairman) (1968) *Report of the Committee on Local Authority and Allied Personal Social Services*, Cmnd 3703, London: HMSO.

Sharpe, L. J. (1967) *Voting in Cities*, London: Macmillan.

Skeffington, A. (Chairman) (1969) *People and Planning*, London: HMSO.

Smellie, K. B. (1968) *A History of Local Government*, London: Allen &
Unwin.
Stoker, G. (1988) *The Politics of Local Government*, London: Macmillan.
Walker, D. (1983) *Municipal Empire*, London: Maurice Temple Smith.
Widdicombe, D. (Chairman) (1986) *The Conduct of Local Authority Business*,
Report and four volumes of research, Cmnd 9797–9801, London: HMSO.
Wood, B. (1976) *The Process of Local Goverment Reform, 1966–1974*,
London: Allen & Unwin.
Young, K. (1986) 'What is Local Government for?', in M. Goldsmith (ed.)
Essays on the Future of Local Government, Wakefield: West Yorkshire
Metropolitan County Council.

Chapter three

Municipal Toryism and Thatcherism

Introduction

During the last decade many Conservative-controlled local authorities on various occasions have found themselves in disagreement and in 'open' revolt against a Conservative central government. These authorities have tended to argue that their opposition to the government's proposals have primarily been their concern to protect local democracy against increased centralism which they see as running against the important Conservative principle of protecting local decision-making against the centralist state. The government's objective on the right of schools to opt out of local authority control is perceived to be a major example of that threat to local democracy.

The leaders of these authorities see themselves as representatives and custodians of the historical traditions of municipalism and the Tory contribution to the growth of local public provision. Tory municipalism implies the upholding of such principles as local political autonomy, the expansion of municipal public welfare and service to the community. In contrast the challenges of Mrs Thatcher's Governments to local government have been increasingly described are being attempts to reject these principles.

Municipalism in the 1980s has been equated with a political opposition, an attempts to resist the priorities set out by a centralist government. Local autonomy and community needs are increasingly running counter to the government's objective of wanting to restrain public expenditure or to deny claims for expanded public services. Furthermore, the principle of collectivism is perceived as being interchangeable with socialism – Mrs Thatcher is seeking to break out of what she calls the ratchet of socialism, by which she means the historical development of public provision and replace these with the ethics of self-help, the individual, family responsibility and voluntary contributions to those in the community who are deemed to be in 'need'.

The aims of this chapter are twofold: first to explore the meaning of the concept of Municipal Toryism, its association with Conservative collectivism and second, to locate this form of Conservative intervention within the context of Thatcherism. Much of the literature on the Thatcher Governments (Keegan 1984; Holmes 1985; Kavanagh 1987) has tended to present Thatcherism as a break with the post-war Butskellite consensus; a strategy which they argue seeks to push back both the frontiers and the costs of government. In contrast, Municipal Toryism is often described as Conservative paternalism, the willingness to deploy public finance to improve individual welfare and a preference for local autonomy to reflect local need.

This chapter questions the perspective that the Conservative Party like the Labour Party, is made up of factions in an uneasy alliance, an uneasy truce between Conservative collectivists and Conservative market liberals each competing to gain ascendancy within the party. Indeed, the aim will be to construct an argument which suggests that the Conservative Party stands for a coherent strategy which is the protection of propertied interests. This means that it continues to ensure that it threads together diverse owners of property into an electoral alliance, identifying their 'common' interests with Conservative administrations.

The combination of arguments outlined here suggest that it would be erroneous to perceive Thatcherism as a break with the traditions of Municipal Toryism. Furthermore, it would be equally misleading to suggest that Municipal Toryism represents local Conservative collectivism. Instead Municipal Toryism embodies choices in political strategies where the continuing priority is the protection of propertied interests. Municipal Toryism needs to be explored as a dual strategy; the strategy of Symbolic Politics where the emphasis is the language of the public interest, symbols of morality, history and nostalgia. The second strategy is the politics of One Nation which in contrast takes seriously the need to construct public policies aimed to creating one nation. However, these forms of politics represent resources rather than factions within the Conservative Party.

The meaning of Conservatism

This section seeks to explore two interpretations of Conservatism; one which sees Conservatism as a form of pragmatic politics. This form of Conservatism is seen as being organicist, aiming to promote universal interests aiming to cement the nation by producing policies which minimize social division, differences in life-styles and opportunities. In contrast there is the approach which suggests that Conservatism inherently represents particularistic interests, namely the interests of those who own property.

Conservative pragmatism points to the nature of Conservatism as being a readiness to reject ideology and an ability to respond according to circumstances (Gilmour 1977; Beer 1965). It is an interpretation of Conservatism which implies that the Conservative Party accepted the need to widen the process of democratic government, whilst recognizing that democracy would increase claims for collectivist welfare. Accordingly the Conservative Party extended the franchise in 1867 and 1884 and also initiated and contributed to continued welfare reform.

This perspective offers two interpretations of Thatcherism. First, there is the argument that the concept of Thatcherism does represent a qualitative break with traditional Conservatism in the sense that it represents a form of politics which takes market liberalism seriously. This approach suggests that Thatcherism involves a restructuring of local economies (Duncan and Goodwin 1988) and a break with the welfare state (King 1987; Gamble 1988). The alternative view suggests that the concept of Thatcherism is completely misleading. Thatcherism represents an emphasis on the rhetoric rather than the reality of policy. According to this approach there has been no qualitative change between the political priorities of the Thatcher Government and Conservative administrations which have preceded her (Pym 1985; Heseltine 1987).

These attempts to evaluate Thatcherism tend the miss the central argument about the true nature of the Conservative Party, which is the protection of property rights and all the assumptions and value judgements which have evolved as a coherent political ideology to protect the interests of property owners. This interest group has obviously continued to expand, but it remains true to suggest that those who see themselves as owners of property are more likely to identify with the Conservative Party as being the party which puts their interests first. These interests include mainly property owners such as business and owner occupiers, but would also include the property industry of conveyancing, estate agencies and institutions involved on housing finance. The Conservative Party since the mid-1870s has continued to represent these specific and particularistic interests but has also strategically sought to expand owner-occupation in housing through mortgage tax relief and more recently by giving large discounts to encourage the transfer of social housing to private ownership.

The attempt to see the Conservative Party as representing a continuing political strategy, disputes the view that the Conservative Party is an empty vessel responding to situations. Instead, Conservative Party leaders seek to construct alliances between individual holders of property, whilst widening the ramparts of property rather than allowing itself to be engulfed by societal pressures. The Conservative Party seeks to give political leadership in the protection of property. It is certainly a view which Lord Salisbury most eloquently emphasized,

> The chief object of Government in England at least, is the protection of property. . . the main business of Parliament is to make laws to define and secure the distribution of property. Finance which has been the main battlefield of so many conflicts, is a contest between various classes waged for the purposes of resisting the imposition of what each considers an unfair proportion of that contribution from property by which the service of the State is carried on.
>
> (Lord Salisbury, 1864, reprinted in P. Smith 1967: 182–3).

Obviously the interests of property are continuously changing. The propertied interests of the late nineteenth century revolved around the industrial capitalist, the house capitalists and the 'shopocracy'. Conservatism, therefore represented the attempt to widen those propertied interests to the ramparts of the nation; hence their aspirations to extend owner-occupation in the inter-war years and after 1950 and the sale of council housing in the 1980s.

There are obvious electoral problems for a party which is particularistic, where this form of particularism serves only the interests of a minority. The question for the Conservative Party is therefore how to win elections in contexts where the interests of property cannot secure a political majority and thus come into conflict with those who seek to improve their well-being through collectivist remedies.

The concept of Municipal Toryism represents the argument that Conservatives need to form an organicist approach to public policy, of governments being capable of representing all interests. However, within these broad aims, the strategy of Municipal Toryism needs to be explored at two levels. At one level Municipal Toryism can be seen as being the need to construct a Conservative hegemony in which the business community, professionals and sections of the middle class are encouraged to become active in their local communities, to seek ways of making communities, whilst preserving the status quo in maintaining political and economic power. We have called this approach Symbolic Politics, in the sense that the aim is to encourage ideas of belonging to the community, that irrespective of income each held a vital role to play. The objective is to improve the well-being of all through thrift, self-help, and hard work.

The second interpretation falls within the category of One Nation Politics. This form of Conservative politics stems from the need to take seriously the problems of governing a two nation Britain where only some enjoy the material fruits of economic prosperity. This approach to Municipal Toryism was embodied in the views of paternalist Conservatives such as Shaftesbury and Disraeli, the Liberal Unionist Joseph Chamberlain and the One Nation Conservatives who joined the Baldwin Government in the 1930s and who continued to dominate Conservative thinking after the Second World War. The common aim of One Nation was that local government should become involved in extensive public works, municipal ownership and income redistribution. It aimed to take Disraeli's thesis of One Nation and construct a programme of social reform. It was a programme which Conservative councils in places such as Leeds, Birmingham, Leicester, and Sheffield were willing to embrace after 1890 in what was defined as a New Era in municipal politics.

Symbolic Politics

Within this framework the values of civic pride, municipal leadership, and making communities were essential elements in seeking to minimize the potential conflict between owners of industries, the new professional middle class and the urban working class. Within this context it was expected that industrialists would show awareness of problems of pollution, housing sanitation and of the benefit of extending education opportunities within local communities.

Municipal pride pointed to the construction of city halls, public libraries, and other public utilities, providing indicators of local success and achievement, a way of threading together business interests with those of the local community. The construction of city halls in 1873 typifies this aspect of Toryism in the sense that these projects were often initiated by private enterprise, by firms coming together and forming a joint stock company. Although many of these buildings were very often jointly financed by the local authority and private enterprise, the aim was to put business at the centre of the community. Queen Victoria's visit to the opening of Leeds City Hall in 1873 reinforced the theme of the strength of free enterprise and the contribution of business to the well-being of local communities. Civic pride meant that business and community had a common interest – the improvement and protection of the locality (Fraser 1979).

Whilst the emphasis was to construct a common interest , this agenda implied the protection of a political status quo, in an environment where economic inequality continued to persist but where those who had economic power were to be made aware of their burden

the articulation of the real interests of those who firstly benefit
from the present structure and who wish to conserve the privileges

they derive from the status quo and second those who prefer
despite exclusion from these privileges what is known and
predictable in the present system and who believe that this how
things should be.

(Norton and Aughey 1981: 47).

This form of Conservatism aimed to promote self-help, reinforcing
family ties when in time of need, expecting the family (women) to care
for the sick, the elderly, and the unemployed. Prosperous members of
the community were expected to make voluntary contributions to their
community by becoming involved in voluntary organizations aimed at
helping the less fortunate and showing the ways to self-help and
self-reliance through charity organizations. Those who had property and
income had a right to these possessions, whilst their contributions to the
community were purely voluntary and altruistic.

The processes of Symbolic Politics were best articulated in the
activities of the Primrose League, a Conservative social movement
which by 1900 boasted a membership of two million right across the
social classes, organized for the primary purpose of taking the
Conservative Party to the newly enfranchised electorate in the 1890s.
By 1900, the Primrose League could point out that their membership in
Bradford was higher than those of the emerging socialist societies, the
birthplace of the Labour Movement. Pugh (1985) describes the
objectives of the Primrose League as seeking to obscure material
distinctions between the worthy, the respectable and the poor and
instead constructing

a feeling of respect and sympathy for the virtues, the struggles and
the aspirations of those born to a life of toil and also to show that
people who by accident of birth are rich or highly placed are not
the soulless selfish beings as depicted by the political stump orator.

(Pugh 1985: 141).

Scruton's (1984) vision of Conservatism corresponds to the political
strategies of the Primrose League in the sense that both the League and
Scruton agree on the nature of the relationship between the state and
civil society. According to Scruton that relationship should be
analogous to that of the family where its members respond to each other
out of love rather than contractual obligation. The state gives the citizen
an identity, a feeling of belonging, of sharing in a community, in public
institutions and traditions. That is all the citizen should expect from the
state

Conservatism arises from the sense that one belongs to some
continuing and pre-existing social order and that this fact is all
important in determining what to do . . . . This feeling, manifest in

patriotism, in custom, in respect for law, in loyalty to a leader or monarch and in the willing acceptance of the privileges of those to whom privilege is granted.

(Scruton 1984: 21, 26)

The Primrose League developed a series of 'local habitations' where members were awarded badges and symbols which evoked a feudal age. The League reinforced the symbols of the monarchy, the church and the Empire. The campaigning style of the League was that of continuous constructions of demonologies, whether it was the threat of the Irish during the debates on home rule in 1890, the preservation of the Empire against its enemies in 1900, or the Communist threat after 1917.

In addition Symbolic Politics encompassed the willingness of the Conservative Party to emphasize sectarian issues as a political strategy aimed to favour the Conservative Party. Waller's (1981) study of Liverpool exemplifies this argument. The Conservative Party dominated Liverpool politics for a century. In years of opposition and retreat the Conservative leadership was driven back upon its denomination support of seeking alliances between Protestants against the Irish Catholic communities of Liverpool. Arthur Forward, the Conservative leader in Liverpool, for example, is found making frequent sectarian speeches after the Liberals had won Liverpool in 1892. Opening the Liverpool Junior Conservative Club in 1893 he claimed that the Liberals were supported only by

the lower strata of society such as the Irish corner rough, too idle to work, too much of an inebriate to find employment and too impecunious to find a permanent home. The influx of the Irish into Liverpool brought poverty, disease, dirt and misery . . . at a cost to the ratepayers of an enormous sum of money ('Hear, hear' said a voice 'What about the Polish Jews?').

(Waller 1981: 141)

The politics of racism and sectarianism represent symbolic forms of politics, because they prioritize communal differences without necessarily providing solutions. They achieve the immediate objective of political victory without policy. However this form of politics is not merely irrational, it also has a material logic for local business interests and ratepayers whose aim it might be to keep the rate to a minimum and therefore that implies the election of Conservative councillors. These interests looked to the Conservative Party in Liverpool, that the Conservative Party was willing to play the sectarian card to widen its electoral base might not have been of importance to these groups, nevertheless if the strategy kept the Conservatives in power and the rates

41

low, then other principles of justice, liberty, and community seemed rather abstract and of low political value.

In the 1880s and up to 1903 the Conservative Party was led by Lord Salisbury who continued to give preference to this form of politics. The Conservative Party under Lord Salisbury had returned from the political wilderness. Salisbury's politics represented the ascendance of a middle-class influence inside the Conservative Party. According to Smith (1967) the middle class had started to desert the Liberal Party in the 1870s alarmed at the radicals within their own party, whilst looking to the Conservative Party as the only party which would protect property interests against high taxation and high rates. Despite their majorities in the House of Commons and their pledges on social reform, the achievements of the Salisbury administrations of the 1890s and Balfour in the 1900s social reform were feeble (Taylor 1975). The strategy of these Conservative Governments was

> to free the energies and support the efforts of an intelligent and industrious people . . . However much you may desire to benefit your neighbour, do not benefit him from taking money out of the pockets of another man.
>
> (Salisbury in Taylor 1985: 157)

There are similarities between the politics of Salisbury and those being espoused by some of the New Right in the 1980s. Throughout his lifetime Salisbury had been a reluctant democrat. He had opposed the Reform Acts of 1867 and 1884, arguing that the Reform Act of 1832 had established constitutional government in Britain. He felt that widening the franchise represented a bribe to the two powerful classes of capital and labour against the interests of those not represented by these organizations, namely the professional middle class, the shopkeepers, and the self-employed. Salisbury described the newly enfranchised Parliament as representing the politics of panic and mere impulses. He anticipated the views of present constitutional liberal thinkers suspicious of the process of democratic government and its impact on individual right to property (Arblaster 1984).

The theme of Symbolic Politics reinforces Smith's conclusion that

> As representatives of property, Conservatives were necessarily opposed to working class claims which trenched upon what they held to be its rights . . . . As politics crystallised along class lines, the Conservatives became more and more a union of propertied interests embattled against organised labour and socialism and largely wedded to the classical liberal tenets of individualism and free enterprise.
>
> (Smith 1967: 324)

One Nation Politics

One Nation Politics stems from the argument that Conservatism is the vehicle of social change and progress, and that Conservatives should not justify inequality and exploitation but work to promote the well-being of the whole nation

the test of inequalities must be the contribution they make to the welfare of society. This justification of inequality is not a justification of the status-quo indeed it implies drastic and radical reforms to secure a socially-responsible capitalism in which inequalities do contribute to public welfare.

(Utley in Cowling 1978: 51)

The concept of One Nation was first to be coined by Disraeli in his attempt to illustrate the impact of industrialism, the problems of urban poverty, and widening social inequality. Disraeli's argument was that leaving the economy to market forces was likely to generate a Britain of two nations: of rich and poor each living in their separate geographical localities and experiencing different lives and expectations. Disraeli felt that a two-nation society would be politically unstable. He advocated a more activist role for the government of becoming interventionist and seeking to produce policies which aimed to construct one nation. The political programme of One Nation, however, had to be initiated by Chamberlain, a Liberal. His aim was to make alliances with Conservative collectivists and permeate the thinking of the Conservative Party. Chamberlain, played an active role in local government during the 1870s. He had given high priority to the issue of pollution control, advocating local government ownership of monopolies such as gas and water supply and suggesting that these profits could be used to promote social welfare. Chamberlain compared the activities of local government to those of a joint stock company

I have always compared the work of a great corporation like this (Birmingham) to that of a joint-stock company, in which the directors are represented by the Councillors of the City, in which the shareholders are every ratepayer and in which the dividends are to be found in the increased health and wealth of happiness and education of the community.

(J. Chamberlain speech in London, 16 July 1906, quoted in Offer 1981: 222)

Chamberlain's programme in Birmingham was imported by most Conservative-led councils after the borough elections of 1890. In places such as Leeds, Sheffield, Edinburgh and Bristol, the local councils showed a great sense of willingness to expand the activities of the authority in areas such as sanitation, health, and education. To finance these services, the authorities resorted to the Chamberlain principle of municipalizing services such as gas, water and the tramways. In Leeds the Conservative council municipalized gas to finance the new budget between 1890 and 1902 (Hennock 1973) and in Sheffield the council municipalized the tramways (Mathers 1979). Municipalism meant that services could be improved without increasing the burden on the ratepayer.

However, this form of Municipal Toryism also met with resistance from local ratepayer movements who argued that the extension of local government, in areas such as municipal house building, would be used to bribe that part of the electorate which was becoming dependent on public provision.

Whilst the politics of Municipal Toryism seemed to be in conflict with the interests and priorities of the suburban middle class and the local shopocracy, these interests were resisted because they were seen as being too narrow. The concerns with 'economy', the level of rates and taxation, had to give way to the wider and truer Conservative objective of creating one nation.

The Association of Municipal Corporations (AMC), established in 1895 under the leadership of Rollitt, a Conservative MP, was an umbrella movement to articulate the creed of municipalism and civic spending. Rollitt, like the Webbs, was a prophet of welfare capitalism but he saw collectivism as a safeguard, not as an alternative, to private property (Young 1975).

Municipal authorities borrowed, invested, and increased rates inexorably after 1890 despite resistance from ratepayer economy movements which were willing to use the Boroughs Fund Act of 1872 to force local polls of the ratepayers. Local authorities became prominent municipal traders competing with private enterprise in the provision of gas, electricity and transport. They were described by the anti-municipalist societies such as the London Metropolitan Society and the Freedom and Property Defence League as being 'a danger to freedom and as sowing the seeds of socialism'.

The election of the Baldwin Government after 1924 brought in Conservatives such as Macmillan, Eden, Boothby, and Chamberlain. It was these Conservatives who were to further the strategy of One Nation in the inter-war-year period and after 1950. As Minister of Health, Neville Chamberlain took the lead with the Housing Act of 1923, Rating and Valuation 1925 and the Local Government Act of 1929, Chamberlain suggested that

> In a democratic State such as ours, with a government which in our time has been made truly representative we together hold the belief

that advantage ought to be taken of the machinery which has thus
been created to do for the people at large, for the whole
community, what no individual can do for himself.

(Chamberlain, July 1906 as quoted in Greenleaf 1983: 241)

The priority which Macmillan set himself in writing *The Middle Way*,
was to show the Conservative Party that the debate about *laissez-faire*
and state intervention was irrelevant in the context of the 1930s. The
British state was already involved in tariff policies, and subsidies to
agriculture and public corporations including the post office, electricity
and gas

a very large proportion of our total wealth production comes under
some form of public utility . . . it is impossible to regard the real
issue of today as being that of a struggle between theories of
laissez faire or state Intervention.

(Macmillan 1938: 173)

State intervention and planning had not produced a socialist or
totalitarian society. It was better to see Britain as a mixed economy,
constructing a middle way between planning for better welfare, whilst
protecting the liberty of the individual. He concluded that only through
continued planning including a programme of economic reconstruction
would Britain resolve the problems of unemployment

we ought to recognise that if it is morally and economically
undesirable, and politically impossible to restore the free market
and free competition, we must adopt the alternative programme of
economic planning.

(Macmillan 1938: 323)

One Nation meant that Conservatives rejected the doctrine of
laissez-faire. Their aim was to form governments which encouraged a
view that people were interdependent, where they had duties as well as
rights. Human nature being what it is, meant that an environment of
laissez-faire was a political choice of government in which the strong
would deny freedom to the weak if they got the chance. The state had to
maintain order, it had to widen opportunities for self-fulfilment, and it
had to care for the casualties. Tories were not afraid to use the power of
the state to foster and preserve individual freedom.

One Nation Conservatism also implied the politics of consent; of
aiming to bring together the main interests of capital, labour, the
government and local authorities into partnerships. Corporatist politics
implied trade union recognition, of establishing conciliation and
arbitration in industrial relations, whilst at the same time trade unions
had to accept the need to give leadership in wage restraint. In return the

role of government was to make the commitment to policies of full employment and improved public welfare. Employers and business had to recognize the need for planning and for more government intervention in investment and wage determination. The overall objective was to create a consensus, a politics of one nation as against narrow and particularistic interests.

According to Gamble (1974) it was the Conservatism of these new progressives which was in ascendance in the immediate aftermath of the Labour victory of 1945. It was R. A. Butler, Ian Macleod, and Macmillan who guided Conservative thinking towards the collectivism that the Labour Government had constructed. Conservatives had to show an equal commitment to the values of universalism in health care, income maintenance and public housing. The Conservative Party had to show that it could manage the economy better, make Britain more prosperous so that better welfare could be guaranteed.

The difference between Symbolic and One Nation forms of politics is best represented in the way exponents perceived the extensions of the franchise and the resolution of the conflict between democracy, property, and the individual. Within the framework of symbolic politics, the extensions of the franchise were not so much a leap in the dark

> than a leap in the dark on an unsuspecting passer-by, the working class voter, by a pack of elitist footpads. The question was not whether the electorate would be beguiled but who would beguile them.
>
> (Waller 1981: 44)

According to this approach Symbolic Politics employs cliches that hint at radicalism, pointing to the need for checking possible abuses of government or other powerful groups against the individual. Symbolic Politics implies 'changing the pump but not the beer' (ibid: 46).

In contrast One Nation Politics accepts that the extension of the franchise and the growth of working class organizations does represent a new form of politics. Accordingly the argument is that the best way of protecting property is to concede on social reform and to construct a form of politics based on the consent of functional groups and interests.

Municipal Toryism and the responses of Thatcherism

Once the meaning of Municipal Toryism is disaggregated, it allows for a better understanding for the context of Thatcherism. First, it would be misleading to continue to argue that Thatcherism represents a break with Municipal Toryism. The suggestion that Thatcherism represented the ascendance of evangelical Conservatives (Keegan 1984) tends to over-emphasize the impact of New Right ideas on the Conservative Party.

This is not to argue that the New Right does not influence Conservative thinking but rather to suggest that the analysis of the New Right has tended to evaluate those ideas concerned with markets, choice and supply-side economics. The New Right however is also very much concerned with the protection of property rights, of the individual rights to property as representing freedom and, of inheritance and income inequality as reinforcing the principles of the market place. The thinking of the New Right is not just directed at ideas of markets but is also associated with the protection of property.

The thesis developed here suggests that Mrs Thatcher is returning Conservative thinking to that which guided the Conservative Party during the years of the Salisbury Government and into the 1930s. That principle was never *laissez-faire* aiming to extend individual choice or a market economy, but more of a politics which aimed to protect specific vested interests such as business, commerce and the middle class, whilst constructing a programme which won elections. The programme of the late nineteenth century, what we called Symbolic Politics, aimed to unite the new enfranchised classes through empire, monarchy and the church against radicals and enemies of British institutions.

Within this context Thatcherism does not represent any form of paradox. The present government might declare a belief in competition but still privatizes public corporations as monopolies. The aim of privatization is not necessarily to to create competition or consumer choice but to shift these industries from the public to the private sector. The Thatcher Governments have proved to be more centralist in their dealings with local government finance, in the reform of education and housing. Historically, the Conservative Party, in the context of financing local expenditure, have always favoured centralist solutions. During the financial crises of 1908, Conservatives supported increases in grant aid from central government to maintain services rather than local taxation, which they felt would hurt local ratepayers. Mrs Thatcher has rejected those proposals which suggest that the financing of local government must guarantee local autonomy. The imposition of the community charge will mean that local government will only be raising some 25 per cent of its own income – the rest will be determined centrally. Furthermore, the community charge will lessen local autonomy.

Thatcherism has also been associated with the language of racism and the empire (Krieger 1986). Mrs Thatcher's speech about blacks swamping the British culture proved to be quite decisive in the 1979 election – it certainly led to the demise of the National Front in some crucial inner-city constituencies. To be 'strong' on race seems to be a good vote winner for the Conservative Party. Immigration 'controls', repatriation, and the mugging of the elderly continue to be ritual debates at the annual conference of the Conservative Party. The argument that the proposals in the 1987 Education Bill – allowing schools to opt out– would lead to racially segregated schools has been defended on the basis of parental choice and if opting out does lead to segregation than so be it.

In addition, Conservative success is still partly explained in Lord Salisbury's reflections, when he suggested it was the existence of Gladstone which provided the greatest source of strength for the Conservative Party. In the context of Gladstone's radicalism, Salisbury saw himself as a policeman in the presence of criminals. People voted Conservative not out of love but for their dislike of the other side. In this context Mrs Thatcher has also continued to remind the British people of the various 'enemies within', including the miners in 1984 and Labour's 'loony left' councils in 1987. The Conservative Party has always managed to portray themselves as the guardians of traditional values, of respecting hard and honest work, thrift, and respect for the police. As Mrs Thatcher was able to claim at the 1988 Conservative annual Conference, the Conservative party is 'camped in the middle of British attitudes and traditions'.

In contrast One Nation Politics represented a perspective which suggested that the context of an emerging organized working class together with a wider franchise required a new form of political settlement. The problem was to what extent would the demands of the labour movement be exceeded to or resisted. Municipal Toryism therefore represented the ascendance of a paradigm which suggested that collectivist welfare represented the best form of resistance to social upheaval. The strategy implied a view which accepted that those who represented the interests of labour had legitimate demands and claims on the state. This form of legitimacy suggested that politics needed to be conducted through the process of dialogue and consent. In this context 'municipalism' meant intervention by local government to improve working-class living conditions, public facilities and to provide better educational opportunities within local communities. Constructing one nation meant increased state intervention and public provision. One Nation Politics rejected the view that one nation could be achieved through the process of market liberalism, a minimalist state and voluntary contributions to charity organizations. One Nation Politics meant the attempt to address tangible social problems rather than appealing to symbols.

The 'statecraft' of Lord Salisbury's four administrations from 1886 to 1903 was to resist the consequences of popular government and the rise of collectivism, and also to construct a politics which limited the role of government. According to Marsh (1978) the primary purpose behind the craft was to curb the excesses and vagaries of popular government.

In more candid moments he [Salisbury] would admit that what he
actually feared was popular demand for heightened levels of
expenditure . . . Then the spectre which had haunted him from his
youth, of a democratic majority recklessly extravagant at the
expense of the propertied minority would become a reality.

(Marsh 1978: 307)

The Salisbury strategy was to question the legitimacy of the narrow
focus of the interests of labour and capital. Instead his aim was to
establish a political framework which defended household ratepayers
and small business. These interests he argued had been increasingly
disenfranchised within the emerging political settlement.

Mrs Thatcher's Governments represent a continuation of the
Salisbury tradition, which is to question, resist, and even defeat corporatist arrangements. However there are some differences between the
1890s and 1980s. The problem for Lord Salisbury was to resist the
emerging demand of collectivism, in contrast Mrs Thatcher has the
problem of controlling, limiting, and, if possible, rolling back that
continuing process of collectivism. The continuity of Lord Salisbury
and Mrs Thatcher has been their readiness to test the strength and
apparent solidarity of the Labour movement. One recognized achievement of the Thatcher years has been to highlight some of the weaknesses
of the labour movement, including its internal struggles, fragmentation,
and the inability to protect public welfare. Collectivism seems to have
been undermined without any political cost to the Conservative Party.
According to Mrs Thatcher there is no such thing as society, but a
society made up of individuals and families.

Conclusions

The history of local government over the last century tends to confirm
the view that Conservative-led councils tended to be municipalists and
also anti-collectivists. However such a statement is too broad – there is
a need to be more specific in answering questions which explain why,
when, and how the Conservative Party moved between these forms of
politics.

During this period four general trends are discernible. First, there is
the period between 1884 and 1910 associated with the new era in local
government. During this period most Conservative councils in the
industrial towns adopted a municipalist strategy; expanding services in
school provision, child medical care, housing, and public health.
Conservative authorities showed great determination in municipalizing
the gas works, water and trams as a way of creating public utilities, but

also as a method for generating profits that would finance public welfare.

The second phase including the period 1910 to 1934 represented a period of retrenchment, a period of local financial crises. The continuing increases in rates inherited from the New Era seemed to reach a saturation level (Offer 1981). The Conservative Party found that it was to their advantage to support such organizations as the London Municipal Society, the National Union of Ratepayers, and the Defence of Freedom and Property League, in their campaigns against the 'march of municipal socialism'. Under the umbrella of the Reform League in London, Conservatives and Liberals were able to deny Labour power within the LCC until 1934, whilst the Progressive Alliance in Edinburgh stayed in power until the mid-1970s.

The unease of ratepayers was articulated at a local level by various 'economist' factions in the various council chambers of Birmingham, Leeds, and Leicester (Fraser 1979) who at one level resisted any form of local state involvement if this was likely to mean higher levels of local expenditure and increased rate burdens on the local butcher, baker, and candlestick maker. However as Fraser has pointed out these 'economists' were not a homogeneous grouping – there was a difference between those who resisted state intervention *per se* and others who wanted to restrain local state intervention

> The fear of increased rates was a perennial obstacle which any
> advocate of an extensive municipal policy had to overcome . . . the
> term 'economists' applied to two distinct features of municipal
> affairs. There was the negative parsimony which was intrinsically
> hostile and which James Holt had associated with Leeds. The
> attitude of Whetstone in Leicester and Avery in Birmingham was
> wholly different. They opposed largess and unnecessary
> expenditure. Both, for instance, advocated municipal ownership of
> water supply. Economists therefore had both a negative and a
> positive public face.
>
> (Fraser 1979: 127–8)

The third phase running between 1934 to the mid-1970s can be described as the era of collectivism, a period when the Conservative Party was dominated by progressives including Neville Chamberlain in the 1930s, Macmillan and Butler in the 1950s, and Heath between 1965 and 1974. These Conservative collectivists accepted the need for social reform, their experiences were the high levels of unemployment and poverty of the 1930s. They accepted the need for central government funding to maintain and improve local services. They were localists in the narrow sense that they did not want Whitehall to dominate the provision of education but were also centralists in their approval of increasing the funding from the centre and thereby reducing the area of autonomy for local government.

The Conservative Party started to disassociate itself from the ratepayer movements – the National Union of Ratepayers Association dismantled in 1934 and the London Municipal Society in 1957. The independence of ratepayers and their criticisms of Municipal Toryism had become an obstacle to the new Conservatism. Party organizers in Smith's Square felt that these organizations had completed their tasks in promoting the interests of the Conservative Party where the party had been previously weak or unpopular. The Conservative Party had become a national party which did not need to encourage ratepayer's organizations or support 'independent' candidates.

The fourth and final phase which can be traced to the mid-1970s, in what might be described as the period of dissatisfaction and self-inflicted crises. In one general sense it parallels the second phase namely that it represents a swing of the pendulum against increased rates and taxation similar to 1910. The attempts to reform the rate support grant (RSG) in the 1960s by introducing the domestic and needs elements together with rate rebates in the 1970s represented strategies to lessen the burden of the ratepayer. However the attempts to reduce public expenditure and consequently the level of RSG in the 1980s have had the paradoxical effects of leading to increases in rate burdens. The commitment by the Conservative Party to abolish rates in the 1970s have become policy in 1987 with the introduction of the community charge.

The community charge (or poll tax) represents a qualitative shift in the *raison d'etre* of local government. Whilst previous governments accepte⁻ that local authorities needed financial assistance to protect ratepayers, under the principle of the poll tax the government is undermining the distributional principle of local rates. The present thinking within the government seems to be that local authorities should confine themselves to deliver a service. The proposals on the poll tax do seem to vindicate the historic resistance of those ratepayers who always felt that public services should be paid for by those who use them. The new beneficiaries of the community charge are likely to be those who presently live in highly rateable properties and who live in single or two person households. The losers are those who at present do not pay rates, who live in low rateable properties, and who have grown up families still living at home.

Within the context of the arguments presented here the thesis that Thatcherism represents a break with Conservative collectivism needs to be qualified. The concept of Thatcherism seems to ignore the centrality of Conservative Party politics, namely its continuing strategy of protecting propertied interests. Conservatism is best understood as a

51

form of politics which seeks to widen property ownership; to make the new owner of the council house feel part an ownership democracy, to identify with the professional middle class of suburbia and the new rich of the shires – to push the ramparts of ownership. In this context Conservative support for municipal reform in the 1890s represented a recognition that their constituency within propertied interests could not guarantee electoral success – they had, in Chamberlain's words, to recognize that property had a ransom to pay to safeguard itself against social revolution. In the shires where the Conservative Party did not have to compete for votes then, it continued to hold down rates without needing to improve services. The child in poverty within the administrative area of the county council suffered far more ill health then his/her counterpart who lived within the boundaries of the corporation.

Thatcherism has often been associated with both the demise of collectivism and also with its continuity. Heroic monetarists such as Hayek and Minford might feel betrayed that this liberal government has not challenged the twin pillars of collectivism. There are at present, despite a third term in office, still no firm plans for shifting the funding of education or health care to the market place. There are obviously common priorities in the politics of liberalism and the Conservative Party and that is the protection of property rights. Under the guise of individual liberty, market liberals support the inequalities generated through property and inheritance. As indicated in this chapter, the Conservative Party continues to be the party of property. It has not however been the party of market liberalism. The proposed reforms in education, housing, and the community charge represent a shift of collectivism towards the centre, where the Conservative Government will ensure that the form of collectivism which is safe is the collectivism which they can control.

References

Addison, P. (1975) *The Road to 1945*, London: Jonathan Cape.

Arblaster, A. (1984) *The Rise and Decline of Western Liberalism*, Oxford: Basil Blackwell.

Bentley, M. (1984) *Politics Without Democracy 1815 to 1914*, London: Fontana.

Beer, S. (1965) *Modern British Politics*, London: Faber & Faber.

Beer, S. (1982) *Britain Against Itself; The Political Contradictions of Collectivism*, London: Faber and Faber.

Blake, R. (1985) *The Conservative Party from Peel to Thatcher*, London: Fontana.

Brittan, S. (1977) *The Economic Consequences of Democracy*, London: Maurice Temple Smith.

Bruce-Gardyne, J. (1984) *Mrs Thatcher's First Administration: The Prophets Confounded*, London: Macmillan.

Bulpitt, J. (1985) *The Discipline of the New Democracy: Mrs Thatcher's Domestic Statecraft*, Papers presented to the Political Studies Association Conference, April.

Butler, (Lord) (1971) *The Art of the Possible*, London: Hamish Hamilton.

Cowling, M. (ed.) (1978) *Conservative Essays*, London: Cassells.

Duncan, S. and Goodwin, M. (1988) *The Local State and Uneven Development*, Oxford: Polity Press.

Fraser, D. (1979) *The Conservative Nation*, London: Macmillan.

Gamble, A. (1988) *The Free Economy and the Strong State*, Basingstoke: Macmillan.

Garrard, J. (1978) *The Middle Class in Politics*, Hants: Saxon House.

Gilmour, I. (1977) *Inside Right, A Study of Conservatism*, London: Quartet.

Greenleaf, W. H. (1983) *The British Political Tradition – The Ideological Heritage*, Vol. II, London: Metheun.

Gyford, J. (1986) 'Diversity, Sectionalism and Local Democracy', in *The Conduct of Local Authority Business*, Cmnd 9801, London: HMSO, Chapter 4.

Hall, S. and Jacques, M. (1983) *The Politics of Thatcherism*, London: Lawrence and Wishart.

Hennock, E.P. (1973) *Fit and Proper Person*, London: Edward Arnold.

Heseltine, M. (1987) *Where There's a Will*, London: Hutchinson.

HMSO (1986) *The Conduct of Local Authority Business – Aspects of Democracy*, vol. IV, Cmnd 9801, London: HMSO.

Holmes, M. (1982) *Political Pressure and Economic Policy*, London: Butterworth.

Holmes, M. (1985) *The First Thatcher Government 1979 to 1983*, Brighton: Wheatsheaf.

Jay, R. (1981) *Joseph Chamberlain – a Political Study*, London: Clarendon Press.

Kavanagh, D. (1987) *Thatcherism and British Politics: The End of Consensus?*, Oxford: Oxford University Press.

Keegan, W. (1984) *Mrs Thatcher's Economic Experiment*, London: Allen Lane.

King, D. (1987) *The New Right: Markets, Politics and Citizenship*, London: Macmillan.

Krieger, J. (1986) *Reagan, Thatcher and the Politics of Decline*, Oxford: Polity Press.

Layton-Henry, Z. (1980) *Conservative Party Politics*, Basingstoke: Macmillan.

Macmillan, H. (1938) *The Midle Way*, Baisngstoke: Macmillan.

Marsh, P. (1978) *The Discipline of Popular Government – Lord Salisbury's Domestic Statecraft 1881 to 1902*, Brighton: Harvester Press.

Mathers, E. (1979) *Sheffield Municipal Politics 1893–1926*, PHD thesis, Sheffield University.

Maudling, R. (1978) *Memoirs*, London: Sidgwick and Jackson.

Norton, P. and Aughey, A. (1981) *Conservatives and Conservatism*, London:

Temple Smith.

Offer, A. (1981) *Property and Politics 1870 to 1914*, Cambridge: Cambridge University Press.

O'Gorman, F. (1986) *British Conservatism*, London: Longmans.

O'Sullivan, N. (1976) *Conservatism*, London: Dent.

Pugh, M. (1985) *The Tories and the People 1880 to 1935*, Oxford: Basil Blackwell.

Pym, F. (1985) *The Politics of Consent*, London: Sphere Books.

Rhodes, James R. (1978) *The British Revolution 1880 to 1939*, London: Methuen.

Rose, R, (1984a) *Understanding Big Government*, London: Sage.

Rose, R. (1984b) *Do Parties Make a Difference*, London: Macmillan.

Rose, R. and Peter, G. (1979) *Can Government Go Bankrupt?*, London: Macmillan.

Scruton, R. (1984) *The Meaning of Conservatism*, 2nd edn, London: Macmillan.

Smith, P. (1967) *Disraelian Conservatism*, London: Routledge & Kegan Paul.

Taylor, R. (1975) *Lord Salisbury*, London: Allen Lane.

Young, K. (1975) *Local Politics and the Rise of Party*, Leicester: Leicester University Press.

Young, K. (1986) 'Party Politics in Local Government: An Historical Perspective', in *The Conduct of Local Authority Business*, Cmnd 9801, London: HMSO, Chapter 3.

Waller, P.J. (1981) *Democracy and Sectarianism*, Liverpool: Liverpool University Press.

Walker, P. (1977) *Ascent of Britain*, London: Sidgwick and Jackson.

Chapter four

Local finance and public expenditure

Introduction

Since the mid-1970s central government has tended to adopt similar policies towards local government finance. The rate of growth in public expenditure has been described as being out of control and in need of closer scrutiny by central government. In addition, the level of public expenditure was becoming a burden on the national economy (Riddell 1983; Jenkins 1987).

The Conservative Governments under Mrs Thatcher have taken this further by adopting the longer term strategy of seeking to reduce the ratio of public expenditure in relation to national income. The Government's plans for public expenditure (HMSO 1988a) into the 1990s show public expenditure growing by 1.25 per cent per annum in real terms, well below the estimated growth in national income. The government's target is for public expenditure to contract to just over 41 per cent of GDP by 1992 – the lowest level since 1972–73. The Autumn Statement of November 1988 showed that the rate of growth in public expenditure during 1988 has slowed further than the government had forecasted in January 1988. Public expenditure in 1988 represents some 38 per cent of GDP (*Financial Times*, 2 November 1988).

By the mid-1970s public expenditure had moved continuously upwards reaching a peak of approximately 50 per cent of national income in 1975. According to the government, expenditure has been brought under control in the 1980s allowing for more resources to be diverted to private consumption, growth in the economy, and higher living standards. The objective the government has set itself is that of achieving 'value for money' in the public sector – eliminating waste and bureaucracy, creating competition for government services, and privatizing services that can be provided by the private sector. To ensure that this strategy will remain in tact in the longer term the government has reduced the rate of personal income tax, thus narrowing the tax base for the funding of the public sector. Future governments wishing to expand public provision will thus have to make the difficult decision to increase the rate of personal taxation.

According to the Layfield Report (HMSO 1976) local government expenditure (including capital and current expenditure) continued to increase throughout the post-war period. In 1950 local authority expenditure comprised some 7.5 per cent of GDP rising to a peak of over 14 per cent of GDP in 1975. The period since 1975 has been characterized by a slowdown in the rate of growth and also a reduction in relation to national income. The Green Paper, *Paying for Local Government* (HMSO 1986), pointed out that local government expenditure in the year 1984/85 had fallen back to 11 per cent of GDP.

The aims of this chapter are threefold: first, there is an attempt to document the various measures taken by central government since 1979 to gain control over local expenditure; second, there is an attempt to interpret the implications of a policy of expenditure control for central – local relations; third we examine the extent to which these changes represent a qualitative break in the financing of local government.

Since 1979, Mrs Thatcher's Governments have continued to control capital expenditure on housing, education, and leisure services by imposing moratoriums on local initiatives. The policy of capital expenditure control has actually led to underspending by local authorities on capital projects (Travers 1986). In contrast the control of current expenditure has as always proved to be more difficult because in this area local authorities do have some degree of autonomy such as increasing domestic rates, increasing charges, and using inherited balances.

Whilst local authorities have throughout the period since 1979 'overspent' the targets set in the government's expenditure plans it must not be assumed that local authorities have been successful in thwarting central government plans. The 'overspend' tended to represent unrealistic targets set by central government rather than the coherent strategy of local authorities. However the Crosland prediction that 'the party was over' has indeed become the reality for local authorities in the 1980s. The taken-for-granted year-on-year growth in expenditure experienced in the previous two decades has been replaced by no growth and retrenchment. Local authorities are no longer involved in creating new areas of policy-making and financial balances tend to get used up quickly in those areas in which local authorities seek to maintain expenditures without increasing rates. Moreover, rate increases tend to hit a saturation point when the local electorate start to feel they are paying more for the same level of services.

The ongoing policy of reducing rate support to local authorities has had a major implication for central – local relations. The potential role of local authorities as initiators and innovators in public policy has been qualitatively eroded. Local authorities have in the 1980s increasingly become agents of central government, delivering a certain level of public provision for a given level of expenditure allocated by central government. Arguments about variation, local needs, and local control over expenditure decisions are no longer part of the policy agenda despite the government's policy objective of freedom of choice. The stated purpose for local government is to give value for money. The role of local government is limited to providing efficient services, where efficiency is often held to be synonymous with reduced costs.

In dealing with the themes of expenditure control and their implications for local government this chapter falls into three main sections. The first section deals with the theme of the politics of public expenditure control and seeks to explain why public expenditure took centre stage in central – local relations. It will be argued here that two interpretations are available to explain government strategy. The first is based on the view that Thatcherite public expenditure policies are derived from public choice theory. In contrast the alternative 'politics of statecraft' model implies a strategy founded on pragmatism and political arithmetic where the government is not driven by doctrinal considerations but with winning the next election. The second section deals with the process of public expenditure control. This section will explain both the changes in public expenditure, and the control of capital expenditure, current expenditure and public sector pay. The third section focuses on the theme of local financial autonomy and shows how the attempt by central government to limit and restrict such autonomy through reductions in the rate support grant and limitations on local authorities scope for raising local rates, culminated in the introduction of the community charge.

The politics of public expenditure control

Public expenditure: the heart of Britain's economic problems

The stated policy objective of the Conservative Government since 1979 has been the reduction of public expenditure, both in real terms and in relation to national income (King 1987). According to Conservative thinking, since the mid-1970s public expenditure and the size of the public sector had been a major determinant in Britain's economic, social, and political decline (Gamble 1988). An inflated public sector had led to high taxes and this has contributed to disincentives to work and to invest; to social malaise, by creating larger numbers of dependents on the public sector; and to increased expectations which governments could not realize.

The medium-term financial strategy (MTFS) which accompanied the

Budget statement of 1980 was the most explicit statement confirming the influence of monetarist perspectives and their impact on public policy (Whiteley 1986). The MTFS represented the acceptance of three highly controversial monetarist propositions. First, the MTFS articulated the argument that the cause of inflation was related to changes in the money supply; second, that the public sector borrowing requirement (PSBR) contributed to monetary expansion; and third, that the reduction in inflation required a reduction in the money supply and hence reductions in the PSBR. The MTFS therefore offered 'paths' for reductions in the money supply, paths for managing the PSBR and inflation.

It is, however, difficult to sustain the monetarist argument that local government expenditure is the cause of inflation. All local government expenditure is 'properly' financed. Local authorities finance their expenditure through loans made by central government or by increasing local rates. This means that local government is not involved in issuing Treasury Bills to the banking sector and therefore, by implication, does not contribute to increases in the money supply and hence, inflation. Furthermore, as Kaldor (1982) was able to show, the main cause of growth in the money supply has been the rate of bank lending to the private sector and not the 'non-funded' (PSBR).

Furthermore, despite these policy projections for the public sector, public expenditure in Britain is still rising as a ratio of GDP. According to the OECD (Mather 1988), public expenditure in Britain in 1986 was still at a higher level than in 1979 when the Conservative Party had come to office. All that the government has managed to do is to bring under control the rate of growth in expenditure experienced during the early years of their own administration. Meanwhile the tax burden has increased from 38 per cent in 1979 to 42 per cent of GDP in 1986.

Justifications for controlling public expenditure were not, of course, derived only from monetarist theories of inflation. Public expenditure and the size of the public sector was also associated with Britain poor economic performance (Bacon and Eltis 1978). From 1976, leading members of the Labour Government had embraced the thesis that public expenditure was connected with resource 'crowding out' (Mullard 1987). Mrs Thatcher's Government took this approach further by suggesting that the size of the public sector exemplified an attempt by government to create dependency on the state, rather than giving people the choice to set their own expenditure priorities. 'Choice' implied less direction by government, it implied the introduction of market principles in areas dominated by public sector monopoly of public provision and, finally, it implied the control of public expenditure in order to leave room for reductions in personal taxation. Only in these ways was it possible that the individual's right to choose could be a reality.

Government endorsement of the dual thesis that the size of the public sector both causes inflation and creates disincentives for self-help and self-reliance, meant that the issue of public expenditure was to become central to policy-making. Constraining and reducing public expenditure held the promise of lower inflation and of freeing resources from public consumption to private investment.

The arguments presented lead us to suggest that central government's concern with local government expenditure needs to be explained at three levels: in terms of political context and in terms of ideology as well in terms of economics. Thus the incoming Conservative Government of 1979 made pledges on health, defence, law and order, pensions and the reduction of taxation. Such a policy mix was incompatible with a policy directed at reducing public expenditure (Pliatzky 1982). The government therefore made the political choice to reduce areas of expenditures which related to local government. Areas such as public sector house building, school maintenance and repairs, environment and roads were relatively easy targets in the policy of expenditure constraint.

However the relationship between central government and local authorities was not confined to the political battle over the control of public expenditure: there were struggles of equal importance about winning the ideological high ground. Local government had, since the late nineteenth century been associated with intervention and collectivism. The Thatcher revolution involved breaking with collectivism and expanding the terrain of individual choice.

The 'politics of statecraft' thesis

A major problem confronting the Thatcher Government in its first term was 'what public expenditures could be reduced?' According to Bulpitt (1987) the Conservative Government was guided by the politics of statecraft – the strategy of seeking and maintaining political power. According to this thesis, statecraft puts a constraint on ideology – the government has to show a willingness to be flexible and to compromise on some policy issues if the political costs are likely to be too high.

> The art of statecraft is to understand and work with the limitations placed on an elite activity by the many changing structural constraints arising from within and without the polity . . . .As a result the story told here can be best regarded as a case study of a successful elite operation in damage control.
>
> (Bulpitt 1987: 183)

According to the statecraft thesis the choice concerning what public expenditure to be reduce therefore depended on the answer to a further question about which areas of public expenditure would be the easier to control – 'easier' being equated with 'minimum political costs'. Reducing expenditure on social housing may be easier because it effects a minority, reducing current expenditure on teachers is potentially more politically costly because such decisions are more directly visible and effect a broader cross section of the electorate.

The 'politics of Thatcherism' thesis

Whilst statecraft implies continuity with the past, as well as compromise and negotiation, the 'politics of Thatcherism' approach suggests the need to take seriously Mrs Thatcher's claims to be a conviction politician. The politics of Thatcherism model argues that 1979 represents a break with the politics of post-war social democracy (Gamble 1988); it is an attempt to restructure the welfare state and hence class relations (Gough 1983) and to construct a 'new realism' around the twin ideas of individualism and self-interest (Offe 1987).

Both models offer prescriptions for the containment of local government finance. The statecraft perspective implies that central government will push on those aspects of local government which will meet with least resistance; thus reducing capital expenditure on public housing and schools would be less politically visible than the closure of a school or an old people's home. The latter are more likely to evoke local alliances for political resistance (Duke and Edgill 1983)

In contrast, the Thatcherism perspective implies 'rolling back' government not just in terms of gross public expenditure but in terms of seeking to divest the public sector of services which the private sector could provide more effectively.

Certainly the measures introduced by central government in the 1980s to control local expenditures have been perceived by some critics of the government as representing a major threat to local government and local democracy – undermining the constitutional foundations of local government and seriously threatening any semblance of local autonomy. Jones and Stewart (1983) in rehearsing the case for local government have argued that local authorities have the right to provide services which local communities vote for. Local government, they argue, is essential to democracy in Britain because it represents the vehicle for local choice and variation, preferences and priorities, and because it symbolizes a bulwark against centralism.

The response of the government to such criticism is to suggest that it is central government which has the primary mandate within the British constitution and that local government is an agent of central government. Conservative thinkers such as Scruton (1984) argue that within the British political tradition, people look to Parliament to make laws – whilst local government is more symbolic than functional. Local government is limited to an administrative role

> financed by local people in order to supply and maintain those services which agreement and tradition had placed in its hands . . . There might even be, as at present a procedure of representation so that those who surrender their money to local administration can see that it is neither squandered nor misapplied.
>
> (Scruton 1984: 163)

The extent to which the politics of Thatcherism represents a break with the post-war consensus rests on how that consensus is defined. The term 'Butskellism' was accurate in the limited sense that both Labour and Conservative Governments during the period 1945 to 1963 had accepted the view that the Budget was an important lever with which to influence economic indicators such as growth and employment. However when it came to welfare there were already in the 1950s sharp contrasts and tensions between Labour and Conservative about the future of collective welfare. Conservatives continued to hold to the theme of efficiency, of targeting welfare to those in need, and continued to be against egalitarianism and universal benefits (Williams 1982).

Again, the Conservative Governments of the 1950s favoured owner-occupation and mortgage tax relief, interest relief on private pensions, and other incentives to occupational welfare. Labour's thinking in contrast was dominated by Crosland's view of socialism, that the classless society was to be achieved through increased state intervention, and continued growth of public expenditure to improve the quality of public sector services. Labour aimed at universalist welfare – the Conservative Party towards selectivity and targeting those in need (Marquand,1988).

The second aspect of the post-war consensus to be questioned by the politics of Thatcherism relate to the dominance of producer groups brought about by the pressures of corporatist politics. Thatcherism represents a break with this kind of functional politics. The 'winter of discontent' in 1979 affirmed to Mrs Thatcher the feeling that local government employees were getting rather 'too big for their boots'. Producer groups seemed too willing to use their clients as pawns in their bargaining with their employers: teachers used parents and children, health workers their patients, and public employees the local community at large.

In the light of this argument, reducing the number of public sector employees represented an attempt to inject market realities into the public sector. Breaking corporatist politics in local government meant undermining the monopoly of trade union producer groups and their cosy arrangements with Labour councils. This form of politics had resulted in profligacy in some Labour-controlled authorities usually at the expense of local ratepayers (Brynin 1988).

This imaging of the public sector fitted in well with the Thatcherite theme of consumer choice. Public sector services were now associated with monopoly, which was often bureaucratic and insensitive to need. To curtail monopoly the government argued that consumer choice, competition and markets needed to become the guiding principles behind local services. Thus council tenants were to be given the right to buy their own homes. Tenants had been 'imprisoned' for far too long in municipal fiefdoms controlled by Labour authorities. Local authorities were also to be encouraged to tender out services such as refuse collection and phase out their direct labour schemes. In education, surrogate market principles were to be introduced, allowing schools to achieve grant maintained status, thus creating competition and choice for parents.

The perspectives of statecraft and Thatcherism are not necessarily mutually exclusive. They are best seen as strategies available to the government. The problem for the Thatcher administrations was how to strike a balance between commitments to the doctrines of markets and 'less government', and at the same time ensuring that the pursuit of doctrine was continuously related to creating political constituencies. So whilst the politics of statecraft was served to control public expenditure between 1979 and 1983, it needed the politics of Thatcherism to explain and underpin forthcoming changes in education, housing, privatization, and local government finance. During the third term of office it can be argued that the government has moved beyond a strategy of controlling local expenditure, to a policy committed to the dismantlement of local forms of collectivism. The policies for the 1990s therefore are designed to change the balance and boundaries between private and public.

The control of local government finance, it can be seen, involves economic, political and ideological considerations. The task for the remainder of this chapter is to disentangle and weigh the impact of each of these factors so that balanced conclusions can be drawn about this aspect of the government's attempt to reform the local authorities.

The control of public expenditure

The aim here to is show how through the process of public expenditure planning, central government gained control over certain areas of public expenditure – those mainly associated with local government. The government succeeded in reducing capital expenditure, although this was already happening during the mid-1970s. Furthermore current expenditure stopped growing after 1983. The control of public sector wage costs was an important factor here (Dean 1981). Although the government had argued against any form of incomes policy, in reality there has been a continuous incomes policy operating within the public sector through the mechanism of cash limits. Since the early 1970s public sector workers have faced the dilemma of either seeking to improve their wages and conditions at the cost of redundancies or lower expenditure on equipment. Within local government, the aim of central government has also been to move away from national agreements to regional bargains which reflect the state of the local labour markets. Finally the attempt to control public sector pay has been further accelerated through the process of competitive tendering.

As already noted the relationship between central and local government has been dominated since 1979 by Whitehall's attempt to gain control over local government expenditure. Expenditures which central government was directly responsible for were constrained by pledges the government had made during the run up to the 1979 election. The government had committed themselves to increasing defence spending, providing new resources for law and order, and maintaining the rate of growth in health expenditure inherited from the outgoing Labour Government. Given these commitments the arena in which the control of public expenditure was going to be lost or won was inevitably within those expenditure areas which were the responsibility of local government.

Analysing changes in public expenditure can take many forms. Within this section expenditure changes are evaluated at two levels: first, through an analysis of changes in individual programmes, and second, by looking at each programme in terms of capital and current expenditure.

Capital expenditure

Table 4.1 provides data for the five major capital expenditure programmes. They constitute some 95 per cent of capital expenditure. The data includes expenditure changes in housing, education, roads, environment, and health. Health is included to show the changing relationship between local expenditure and central government expenditures. The table includes data for the period 1967 to 1987. The data has been deflated by the appropriate capital deflator and all prices are shown using the 1985 price series as used in the latest edition of the *United Kingdom National Accounts* (HMSO 1988b). The first remark to be made is that capital expenditure as a percentage of GDP has continued to fall since 1969. In 1969 total capital expenditure represented some 4.1 per cent of GDP; in 1979 this had fallen to 2 per cent, and by 1987 capital expenditure constituted some 1.3 per cent. Total capital expenditure in 1974 was around £12 bn, in 1987 this had fallen to £4.8bn. However these general trends do not mirror what was happening at the individual programme level. In housing, for example, capital expenditure was not in continuous decline, but actually expanded between 1970 and 1974. The Heath Government had used housing capital expenditure as a macroeconomic lever to reduce unemployment. Since 1975 housing capital expenditure has fallen very steeply from 1.8 per cent of GDP to 0.3 per cent in 1987. Housing capital expenditure has taken the brunt of expenditure reductions. Capital expenditure on education seems to follow the trend for total capital expenditure. It seems that there has been continuity of policy – of giving low priority to school repairs and maintenance since 1970. In 1971 education expenditure consisted of 0.6 per cent of GDP or £1.5bn; in 1987 this had fallen to 0.2 per cent of GDP or £0.7bn. In contrast capital expenditure on health has actually risen since 1979. During the years of the Labour Government, health capital expenditure fell from from 0.34 per cent of GDP to 0.24 per cent of GDP in 1978. Since 1979 capital expenditure on health has continued to rise.

Table 4.1 Capital expenditure by programme and total expressed as percentages of GDP (market prices) deflated by the domestic fixed capital deflator

Year	Housing	Education	Health	Roads	Environment	Total
1967	1.9	0.6	0.3	0.9	0.7	4.1
1969	1.7	0.6	0.3	1.0	0.7	4.3
1971	1.2	0.6	0.3	1.0	0.9	4.0
1973	1.2	0.7	0.4	1.0	1.0	4.2
1975	1.8	0.5	0.3	0.8	0.5	3.8
1977	1.2	0.3	0.3	0.5	0.3	2.6
1979	0.8	0.2	0.2	0.4	0.3	2.0
1981	0.2	0.2	0.4	0.3	0.3	1.4
1983	0.4	0.2	0.3	0.5	0.3	1.7
1985	0.4	0.2	0.3	0.5	0.1	1.4
1987	0.3	0.2	0.2	0.5	0.1	1.3

Source: United Kingdom National Accounts (1975 onwards) Tables 1.6, 1.7, and 9.4.

Taking capital expenditure as a whole, therefore, we can confirm that this component of public expenditure has been drastically reduced. However this trend obscures some important changes at the programme level. Separating capital expenditure according to central/local government responsibilities, it has been local government expenditure which has been reduced with housing experiencing the sharpest reductions. In contrast health capital expenditure has been rising since 1979 confirming the Thatcher Government's claims that it was the Labour Government which had cut the hospital building programme and that the Conservatives are now building more new hospitals.

Current expenditure

Within our analysis of current expenditure are included those expenditures which together make up 95 per cent of total current expenditure. Thus, within this category we include defence, law and order, and health as central government expenditures. In contrast, expenditures on roads, education, environment/leisure, and personal social services (PSS) are defined as local government services.

Between 1979 and 1987 total current expenditure fell from 17.8 per cent of GDP to 16.7 per cent. However it is important to note that the control of current expenditure did not start seriously until 1985. Between 1980 and 1984 current expenditure was continuously rising from 17.6 per cent in 1979 to a peak of 18.8. per cent in 1983.

In contrast to capital expenditure, current expenditure is always more difficult to control. On capital expenditure local authorities have to submit their capital expenditure schemes to the public loans board for approval, thus making it easier for central government to scrutinize, approve and issue moratoriums on capital expenditure. With respect to current expenditure local authorities tend to have more leeway because such expenditure can be financed through increases in local rates. Furthermore, current expenditure supports wages and employment in the public sector which is often more politically difficult to cut than capital expenditures.

There is a significant contrast to be drawn in looking at individual expenditure programmes. Central government expenditure on defence, law and order, and health has been expanded throughout the period 1980 to 1987 (see Table 4.2). In 1987 expenditures on these programmes was higher than when the Conservatives came to office in 1979 (except for defence expenditure which seems to have been brought under control in 1987). These expenditures represent the election pledges made by the government. In contrast expenditure on roads, environment, and PSS has actually fallen, whilst for education – which has the highest component going to wages and salaries – expenditure has been held constant. For all the programmes which are the main concern of local government the level of expenditure is always lower in 1987 than it was in 1979. Thus whilst education expenditure was taking some 4.9 per cent of GDP in 1975, in 1979 this had fallen to 4.0 per cent and in 1987 it is still at same level as in 1979. Expenditure on the environment and leisure services has declined drastically from 1.1 per cent of GDP in 1979 to 0.4 per cent in 1987.

Table 4.2 Current expenditure by programme and total expressed as percentages of GDP (market price) using the central government consumption deflator

Year	Defence	Law	Education	Health	Environment	Roads	Trade	PSS	Total
1967	7.3	1.3	4.1	4.4	1.4	0.9	0.7	0.2	17.8
1969	5.8	1.2	3.8	4.1	1.0	0.7	0.8	0.3	17.7
1971	5.5	1.3	3.9	4.2	1.0	0.7	0.8	0.4	17.9
1973	5.4	1.4	4.1	4.2	1.1	0.7	0.7	0.5	18.1
1975	5.1	1.5	4.9	4.8	1.3	0.7	0.7	0.6	19.6
1977	5.0	1.5	4.2	4.6	1.1	0.7	0.7	0.6	18.3
1979	4.9	1.5	4.0	4.5	1.1	0.7	0.7	0.6	17.8
1981	5.2	1.7	4.2	5.1	1.0	0.7	0.5	0.7	19.1
1983	5.2	1.7	4.0	5.0	1.1	0.6	0.5	0.7	18.8
1985	5.1	1.6	3.9	4.7	1.2	0.5	0.4	0.8	17.4
1987	4.4	1.7	4.0	4.7	0.4	0.5	0.4	0.7	16.7

Source: *United Kingdom National Accounts* (1975 Onwards) Tables 1.6, 1.7, and 9.4

The control of wage costs in the public sector

In addition to the control of public expenditure through mechanisms such as the Public Expenditure Survey Committee (PESC) and legislation on rate-capping, central government has tried to give a lead to local authorities, as employers, in pay bargaining with local authority workers. The Thatcher approach has in a sense been no different to that of previous administrations. The government continues to believe that there is a need to give a lead on pay to the private sector. The belief is that government pay bargains tend to set the lead for workers in the private sector. Despite official utterances that this government does not need an incomes policy, the government does seem to operate one as far as the public sector is concerned. Using the mechanism of cash limits central government assumes a level of inflation for pay settlements and then allows local authorities, public corporations and health authorities to bargain with their workers within these parameters (RIPA 1985). If public sector workers seek to break with cash limits then they are either faced with redundancies or with less expenditures on other resources.

The problem of attempting to control public sector pay is that the success of such a policy has always proved to be short term – with public sector workers eventually 'catching up' with their private sector counterparts. The Clegg awards of 1979, for example, tended to re-dress some of the problems in the public sector created by three consecutive years of pay policy during the years of the Labour Government. From 1980 to 1982 public sector pay settlements did fall behind the private sector, but there was already evidence of them catching up by 1984. Again in 1986 public sector pay settlements had fallen behind the private sector, but latest estimates for 1987–8 again show that public sector workers have been closing the gap during 1988 (HMSO 1988c).

Furthermore, the highly politicized context of local government in the 1980s has made pay bargaining for local authority workers more difficult to operate within the constraints of cash limits, because of the fragmentary nature of the local authorities as employers. The swing to the Labour Party in local government control since 1980 has meant that Labour has gained control of the Association of Metropolitan Authorities (AMA) and the Association of District Councils (ADC), leaving the Conservatives and the Alliance in control of the Association of County Councils (ACC). Labour employers have tended to allow for higher pay awards for local authority manual workers, thus forcing Conservative employers to follow. In 1986 local authority manual workers negotiated a 10 per cent pay rise whilst other public sector workers were negotiating agreements of around 6 per cent. In 1987 the Labour-controlled authorities allowed for pay increases of 10 per cent.

The government's response to these local pay awards has been twofold. First there has been exhortation in the speeches in late 1986 and 1987 by the, then, Paymaster General Kenneth Clarke. Clarke's argument was that there was no need for national agreements and he urged local authorities to break away from these bargaining forums and move to local agreements which could reflect wider local labour market conditions. Conservative authorities such as Westminster, Lincoln, and Worcester have been at the forefront of this policy. The paradox for decentralized agreements is that many local authorities in the south and south east are finding it increasingly difficult to attract managers and professionals and are finding themselves in increased competition with banks, insurance companies, and building societies. To maintain recruitment of professionals, local authorities are being forced to offer inducements on mortgages, relief on cars, and higher pay awards.

Competitive tendering

Second, the government has used compulsory tendering as a strategy for holding down public sector pay (Low Pay Unit 1987; Ascher 1987). Local authority workers seeking to win in-house contracts but faced with high overhead costs have had to dampen their wage demands to make their bids more successful. Compulsory tendering and privatizing services will obviously make it even more difficult for local authority workers to win contracts.

The Local Government Act of 1987 which came into effect in July 1988 obliges local authorities to extend competitive tendering to six areas of local government service: street cleaning, building cleaning, vehicle maintenance, refuse collection, grounds maintenance, and catering. The problem now facing local authority manual workers is how to reduce their overhead costs, such as administration, payroll costs, computing, legal services, and printing if they are to make a competitive in-house bid. These services are utilized by other groups working for the local authority: How are they to be apportioned, would it better to purchase them elsewhere?

Whether the tender is won in-house or goes to the private sector the net result will be the same. Competitive tendering tends to result in lowered conditions of service and lower pay. Local authority manual workers at the end of the day will have to compete with their counterparts in the private sector, often working for private sector firms with lower overhead costs, lower wages and poorer conditions of service. The experience of private tenders to date tends to indicate that the cost of a private tender is always about 20 to 30 per cent cheaper than the in-house application. Using the sole criteria of value for money it would seem highly likely that tenders for these contracts will be won by the private sector.

Reducing the financial autonomy of local government

Whilst public expenditure levels are decided at the centre through the mechanisms of PESC and expenditure white papers, local government still has some autonomy in deciding the levels of local expenditure through its determination of local rates. The attempt to control local expenditure has led central government into an arena long seen as being the responsibility of the local authority and their local electors preferences. This section therefore seeks to examine the attempt by central government to reduce the financial autonomy of the local authority. Strategies employed include the introduction of the grant related expenditure (GRE), penalties, rate-capping, abolition and the introduction of the community charge.

Controlling domestic rates

Historically the rating system has led to local variation in the provision of services. Local authorities and local communities through the process of local elections have had the choice to improve local services or provide new services through the rates. The Conservative Party and Conservative Governments have argued since the mid-1970s that the rates were regressive on single-person households, that local services were not being paid for by those who enjoyed them and that local business was disenfranchised from the process of local elections. Local elections were therefore increasingly seen as not providing an appropriate mandate for rates increases. Those who did not pay any rates had a vested interest in voting for more services, knowing that the costs would be paid by others.

Since 1979 the issue of local rates has become more acute for the Conservative Government. Mrs Thatcher had pledged in 1979 that she would abolish rates. A Green Paper in 1981 – 'Alternatives to Rates' – actually confirmed the findings of Layfield in 1977, namely that local rates were an efficient form of local tax, easy to collect, cheap to administer and giving predictable yields. Local rates preserved forms of local autonomy and if rates were to be abolished then they would have to be replaced by some form of local income tax. Patrick Jenkin, the Secretary of State for the Environment, had to tell a disheartened Conservative conference in 1983 that there was no real alternative to the rates.

Government intervention to protect ratepayers during this period took various forms. First there was the proposal by Michael Heseltine, Secretary of State for the Environment, to hold local referendums on rate increases – this proposal was however abandoned by Heseltine after opposition from the House of Lords on the basis that the government was trying to meddle too much with local autonomy. Heseltine did, however, go on to make it illegal for local authorities to raise a supplementary rate.

During the early 1980s the government also introduced the concepts of block grant and grant related expenditure (GRE) into the workings of the rate support grant (RSG). This meant the 'needs' element which had evolved since the mid-1960s as a mechanism to redistribute grant to those areas which experienced special problems became part of a package to be decided at the centre. From the mid-1980s the Department of the Environment took on the task of deciding the level of need appropriate to each local authority. The GRE was supposed to reflect local need.

The government introduced two financial targets for local authorities; a GRE target which indicated to the authority what they ought to be spending and an expenditure target which confirmed their current spending levels. For most authorities in the shire areas, and some metropolitan districts, the GRE target was above their expenditure target. This meant that these authorities were provided with opportunities to increase their expenditure. The only authorities which were spending above their GRE targets were the Labour-controlled authorities in London – areas with high levels of multiple deprivation which the GRE target seemed to underestimate – and these authorities attracted a high level of penalty and RSG claw-back. In 37 out of 40 shire counties the GRE was higher than the disciplinary target, allowing for an increase in expenditure of £463m, whilst in the metropolitan areas, 17 out of 42 councils had a higher GRE. These estimates suggested paradoxically that the government was encouraging local authorities to increase spending!

Realizing that the GRE and disciplinary targets might legitimize increased spending, the government moved the goal posts by reassessing the GRE targets in 1981. Many Labour authorities such as Hackney and Lambeth were faced with penalties of £3.2m as were Conservative authorities in Avon and Nottinghamshire. The problem for the government was that under the Planning and Land Act of 1981, the government had declared that the GRE calculation would only be used to increase grant. The reassessed GREs therefore made it illegal for the government to reduce grant. This was corrected by the Local Government Finance Bill of 1982 which contained a new clause allowing the government both to increase and reduce the multiplier.

The total sum of these changes was obvious confusion for the local authorities. Local authority finance officers were forced to abandon any form of local planning for house building or other long-term projects. According to the leader of Hackney Council

> Planning ahead is wholly impossible. Housing allocations come late, the grant figures are late, grant is being adjusted almost weekly and just when you think everything is tied up you find it isn't. They make the rules of the game, we fight and then decide to play. Half way through the first half Heseltine tries to move the bloody goalposts.
>
> (John Kotz, *Financial Times*, 16 March 1982)

The system of targets and penalties was eventually abolished in 1985. Instead of encouraging control of expenditure, the system seemed to have had the opposite effect. The authorities which spent to their new GRE target attracted higher grant from central government whilst those authorities which continued to pursue 'good housekeeping' actually lost grant. The government seemed to be encouraging the overspenders.

The system of penalties was replaced by the provisions of the Rates Bill of 1983 which introduced the system of a statutory rate (or rate-capping) for specific local authorities. The government maintained that a handful of local authorities were deliberately breaking with the historic convention of local authorities abiding by central government in the direction of economic policy. Rate-capping was seen by many critics as being the final attempt to turn local government into a form of local administration – delivering services on behalf of, and as defined by, central government, limiting council's freedom to determine their own levels of expenditure and taxation. Several prominent Conservative MPs were unhappy with the proposal which seemed to undermine a 400-year-old right for local authorities to determine their own rates level. Anthony Beaumont Dark argued that

If this Bill is only to be used against the few admittedly zany authorities then it is unnecessary. If it is to be used like a gun to demand in the end the unconditional surrender of local powers to central dictat than it is the most retrograde piece of legislation ever introduced by a Conservative Government.

(Financial Times, 14 January 1984)

Besides the resistance of Conservative MPs, leaders of Conservative authorities on the ACC and the ADC – both Conservative-controlled – had equally been very upset with the bill and described it as a threat to local democracy. Mrs Thatcher seemed to threaten the Conservative local authority leaders on the ACC who withdrew prepared press statements and also declined to appear as scheduled on a BBC programme during the House of Commons debate on the bill . Mrs Thatcher seemed to have given sufficient reassurance that only 12 authorities would be effected and that these were the 'hard left' Labour authorities.

Rate-capped authorities were to be named in the House of Commons with the Secretary of State detailing the local rate level for each of the authorities listed. Any authority which increased rates above that level were deemed to be *ultra-vires* and could be taken to court by local ratepayers and the Secretary of State. The rate-capped authorities continued to be, in the main, London Labour-controlled authorities, although sometimes authorities such as Portsmouth found themselves on the hit list of high spenders.

The attempt to control local government expenditure had proved to be quite effective. Whilst in each year since 1981 local authorities had continued to overspend their targets by £1bn – this only represented some 0.5 per cent of total expenditure. Within some authorities the reductions in capital and current expenditure were being financed increasingly through the rates where the introduction of a GRE, disciplinary targets, and penalties had only resulted in breaking the link between local expenditures and local rates.

The 'failure' by local authorities to meet the government's targets were more the result of underestimating inflation, and the length of time it took for authorities to adjust their expenditures, than any coherent attempt to undermine the government's economic policy.

The 1986 RSG settlement allowed for local authority expenditure to rise in line with the rate of inflation. This meant an increase in planned expenditure for local authorities for the year 1987–8 of £3.4bn. The *Financial Times* editorial concluded,

> So after years of creating havoc in the town hall finances, and weakening local accountability by breaking the link between expenditure rises and rates rise, the Government has chosen to restore the link and introduce much needed stability.
>
> (*Financial Times*, 23 July 1986).

Abolishing the GLC and metropolitan counties

During the 1983 election the Conservative Party also committed itself to abolishing the Greater London Council (GLC) and the six metropolitan county councils (MCCs). According to the government, this represented an attempt to streamline the cities, to bring local government closer to local communities, and to curb by authorities which had no identifiable local obligation. The government also argued that abolition would bring savings of approximately £1bn.

The case for savings was questioned by the management consultants Coopers and Lybrand and also Travers, who in his attempt to test the government's claim of savings, was forced to conclude,

> Don't believe any claims by government or opposition. The costs have been divided between so many organisations using different accounting methods that the answer will never be known.
>
> (*Financial Times*, 1 April 1987)

What abolition did achieve was the transfer of waste disposal, police and fire service from locally accountable authorities to *ad hoc* non-elected bodies. Again, new employment initiatives developed by Greater London Employment Board (GLEB) in London and the West Yorkshire Employment Board (WYEB) became dependent for their funding on the goodwill of the London boroughs and district councils. A tier of local government which was to be a bulwark against centralism had proved to be too much of a nuisance for central government!

Introducing the community charge

The proposals for a community charge (or poll tax) had been examined in the Green Paper 'Alternatives to Domestic Rates' in 1981 and had been, according to Robin Pauley of the Financial Times, rejected by the government as a viable option. Pauley was able to confidently predict that

> the disadvantages of a poll tax, including the ease with which it could be avoided, means it is likely to be a strong contender but

fall before the finish. If electoral rolls were to be used for the purposes of levying the tax there would almost certainly be strong resistance in Parliament and from the civil liberties lobby, a fact which had already turned the Home Office against any such idea.

(Financial Times, 17 December 1981)

However, despite the Green Paper of 1981 and the 1983 speech by Patrick Jenkin to the Conservative conference in which he expressed the view that local rates represented the best form of local tax, concern in the Conservative Party about local authority finances had reached a peak with the rates revaluation in Scotland in 1985. The local election results of that year were a disaster for the Scottish Conservative Party. Rates revaluation in England held the potential of producing similar results. The Green Paper 'Paying for Local Government' proposed the community charge as the only real alternative to domestic rates. The idea of introducing a tax on individuals irrespective of their housing conditions and personal income was seen by many as such a radical shift in thinking (with so many winners and losers) that it was unlikely to be translated into action.

The change from local rates to the community charge implied the end of local rates as a form of income redistribution. As far as the government was concerned local government exists only to deliver a public service, and to be accountable to those who pay for these services. As far as income redistribution was concerned, this was achieved via income tax. The principle of the community charge was, therefore, to rest on a charge on individuals. That principle was to be safeguarded in the House of Lords debate in June 1988, when Conservative whips in the House of Lords ensured the highest turn-out of Conservative Lords to defeat an amendment which would have introduced the concept of ability to pay. That amendment would have inflicted a heavy defeat on the community charge. The readiness of the government to use their inbuilt majority in the Lords showed the level of seriousness of the government to carry through the principle of the community charge.

Besides removing the mechanism of income redistribution at a local level, the community charge and its capping mechanisms would ensure that in future local authorities would lose their autonomy in defining local needs. Even if local communities decide to vote for better services and a higher community charge, the gearing ratio between loss of grant and increases in the charge will be too high to contemplate better services.

Conclusions

Despite the apparent inconsistency in dealing with local government finance there have been discernible common trends and a certain coherence in the government's policies towards local authorities. The central objective of the government has been to gain thorough control over the rate of growth in public expenditure. The government wants public expenditure to take a decreasing ratio of national income; growth in the economy must no longer necessarily imply new or increased resources for the public sector. Rather than maintain public sector expenditure as a stable ratio of GDP, it is planned to fall continuously into the 1990s (Autumn Statement, November 1988).

Alongside this overall strategy, therefore, growth in the economy will be used by the Treasury to reduce the public sector debt and/or or reduce personal taxation. The pledge to reduce personal taxation to 25 pence (and 40 pence for those earning above £19,000) has cost the Treasury some £3bn in 'lost' revenue which would have otherwise been available for improved public sector services. Having achieved the target of 25 pence in the third term of office the Chancellor has set a new target of 20 pence for future Conservative administrations.

Within this overall context of a reduced public sector the control of public expenditure is decisive. Despite public sector financial surpluses and forecasts of growth in the economy of 4 per cent, the Chancellor was able to announce that the total for public expenditure during the year 1989–90 will be held to the planned total agreed in January 1988. Despite resistance and unease amongst some Conservative MPs about the freezing of child benefit or the introduction of charges for eye testing and dental inspections, the government has shown no signs of compromise, although as suggested above, the control of local expenditures has always seemed to be an easier and safer political venture for the government. The control of capital expenditure on housing, roads, and environment had already been tested by the Labour Government in the mid-1970s and had met little local resistance. The Conservative Government in 1979 could therefore declare that their policy on capital expenditure was no different to that of the outgoing Labour Government. The sale of council housing and the introduction of moratoriums on public housing in 1981 did not result in unpopularity for the government. And despite the lengthening of council waiting lists, reports on homelessness and the deprivations of bed and breakfast accommodation, Mrs Thatcher was actually able to divert the blame for these difficulties onto local authorities, for underspending their capital budgets.

In addition, it might be argued that the attempt to control local authority finance represented a journey for the government rather than a coherent strategy. The government seemed to be 'learning on the job' in introducing new measures to Parliament. The Local Government Planning and Land Act 1980 was introduced during the first session of Parliament followed by the introduction of GREs. Despite opposition from Conservative MPs who saw the government policy as threatening local democracy (and similar forms of unhappiness in the House of Lords), each of these measures was passed into legislation without challenges to their central principles. This was repeated after the 1983 election with the introduction of the Rates Bill and the proposals to abolish the GLC and MCCs. Again Conservative opposition, ultimately ineffective, concentrated on the loss of local democracy. The third phase, which started in 1987 introduced the community charge, an Education Bill, a Housing Bill and a Local Government Bill all in the first parliamentary session. Opposition again concentrated on the loss of local democracy, the danger of centralism and even the threat of an 'elective dictatorship'. However the community charge principle has remained in tact.

Let us return to the question posed at the beginning of this chapter. Our review of public expenditure policies seems to confirm that the use of the concept of Thatcherism is appropriate in the context of local government finance. There is little evidence to show a willingness to compromise by the government, instead experience shows a single-minded commitment to alter the dynamics of local government finance, whether by cutting central government grants, using competitive tendering to reduce labour costs, or introducing the community charge to remove local government financial autonomy.

The idea of the 'politics of Thatcherism' has been used in this chapter to indicate that the Conservative Governments from 1979 have embarked on a coherent strategy aimed to break with the post-war consensus about the growth and expansion of local public provision, and to establish a new form of politics. In the context of local government finance it is clear that the government has embarked on a process to radically alter assumptions about local services, how these are financed, and by whom they are delivered.

The abolition of local domestic rates, to be replaced by a community charge in 1990, means that in future local government will exist for the narrow purpose of delivering services. The community charge removes the ability of local authorities to redistribute income and dramatically limits their ability to adjust services according to community needs. More broadly, Thatcherism is committed to undermining collectivism, and to the advancement of individual self-reliance. The government has sought to give individuals the right to keep and dispose of more of what they earn; and to widen the areas of choice for the disposal of private income – on private education and personal insurance, for example.

Collectivism is no longer seen as the route for advancing the citizen's quality of life. The way forward lies in the promotion of a responsible individualism, one which encourages people to take responsibility for their families and, through charities and philanthropy, for their fellow citizens who are less fortunate.

References

Arestis, P. (1984) 'The UK Monetarist Experiment' *Journal of Public Policy*, 4: 39–56.

Ascher, K. (1987) *The Politics of Privatisation*, Basingstoke: Macmillan.

Asociation of County Councils (1983) *Rates, The Way Ahead*.

Association of Metropolitan Authorities (1983) *Rates Limitation, Summary of the AMA Response*.

Bacon, R. and Eltis, W. (1978) *Britain's Economic Problem: Two Few Producers*, London: Macmillan.

Behrens, R. (1980) *The Conservative Party from Heath to Thatcher*, Farnborough: Saxon House.

Boyson, R. (1978) *Centre Forward: A Radical Conservative Programme*, London: Temple Smith.

Breton, A. (1974) *The Economic Theory of Representative Government*, London: Macmillan.

Brittan, S. (1977) *The Economic Consequences of Democracy*, London: Temple Smith.

Brynin, M. (1988) *The New Urban Left: A Contemporary Folk Devil*, paper presented to the Political Studies Association Conference, April.

Bulpitt, J. (1987) 'Thatcherism as Statecraft', in M. Birch and M. Moran (eds) *British Politics: A Reader*, Manchester: Manchester University Press.

Conservative Central Office (1977) *The Right Approach to the Economy*, London: Conservative Party.

Dean, A. (1975) 'Earnings in the Public and Private Sector 1950 to 1975', *National Institute Economic Review*, November: 60–7.

Dean, A. (1981) 'Public and Private Sector Pay and the Economy', in J.C. Fallick and R.F. Elliott (eds) *Incomes Policy, Inflation and Relative Pay*, London: Allen & Unwin.

Duke, V. and Edgill, S. (1983) *Public Expenditure Cuts in Britain and Consumption Sectoral Cleavages*, paper presented to the Political Studies Association, April.

Gamble, A. (1988) *The Free Economy and the Strong State*, Basingstoke: Macmillan.

Gough, I. (1983) 'Thatcherism and the Welfare State' in S. Hall and M. Jacques (eds) *The Politics of Thatcherism*, London: Lawrence & Wishart.

Heald, D. (1983) *Public Expenditure*, Oxford: Martin Robertson.

HMSO (1976) *Committee of Inquiry into Local Government Finance*, Cmnd 6453, London: HMSO.

HMSO (1977) *Local Government Finance*, London: HMSO.

HMSO (1981) *Alternatives to Domestic Rates*, London: HMSO.

HMSO (1983a) *Streamlining the Cities*, Cmnd 9063, London: HMSO.
HMSO (1983b) *Rates*, Cmnd 9008, London: HMSO.
HMSO (1984) *The Local Government Bill*, London: HMSO.
HMSO (1986) *Paying for Local Government*, Cmnd 9714, London: HMSO.
HMSO (1988a) *The Government's Expenditure Plans 1988–89 to 1990–91*, vol. 1, Cmnd 288, London: HMSO.
HMSO (1988b) *United Kingdom National Accounts*, London: HMSO.
HMSO (1988c) *New Earnings Survey 1988*, Part A, London: HMSO.
House of Commons (1984) *Local Government: The Rate Limitation Report 1984*, House of Commons Paper 589, London: HMSO.
Jenkins, P. (1987) *Mrs Thatcher's Revolution: The End of a Socialist Era*, London: Jonathan Cape.
Jones, G. and Stewart, J. (1983) *The Case for Local Government*, London: Allen & Unwin.
Kaldor, N. (1982) *The Scourge of Monetarism*, Oxford: Oxford University Press.
King, D. (1987) *The New Right: Politics, Markets and Citizenship*, Basingstoke: Macmillan.
Labour Research Department (1987) *Privatisation: Paying the Price*, London: LRD.
Layton-Henry, Z. (1980) *Conservative Party Politics*, London: Macmillan.
Low Pay Unit (1987) *Cleaning and Caring*, Leeds: West Yorkshire Low Pay Unit.
Marquand, D. (1988) *The Unprincipled Society: New Demands and Old Politics*, London: Jonathan Cape.
Mather, G. (1988) *Government By Contract*, paper presented to Royal Institute of Public Administration Conference, Kent University, September 1988.
Mullard, M. (1987) *The Politics of Public Expenditure*, London: Croom Helm.
Offe, C. (1987) 'Democracy Against The Welfare State', *Political Theory* 15(4): 501–37.
Pliatzky, Sir Leo (1982) *Getting and Spending*, Oxford: Basil Blackwell.
Riddell, P. (1983) *The Thatcher Government*, Oxford: Martin Robertson.
RIPA (1985) *Implementing Government Policy Initiatives, The Thatcher Administration 1979 – 1983*, London: Royal Institute of Public Administration.
Scruton, R. (1984) *The Meaning of Conservatism*, London: Macmillan.
Travers, T. (1986) *The Politics of Local Government Finance*, London: Allen & Unwin.
Whiteley, P. (1986) *Political Control of the Macro-Economy*, London: Sage.
Williams, P. (1982) *Hugh Gaitskell*, Oxford: Oxford University Press.

Chapter five

Public services and Thatcherism

For over half a century local government in Britain has exercised key responsibilities in shaping and delivering a range of welfare state services. While Westminster and Whitehall have imposed overall policy frameworks, and provided a significant element of central funding, local authorities have been allowed an operational autonomy to shape services in accordance with the needs of their areas and the aspirations of the people who live in those areas. This model of central-local relations – of a 'non-executant' central administration (Dunleavy and Rhodes 1986) working in a 'hands-off' partnership with a local government system that is allowed to get on with the task of providing important educational, housing, welfare, and other services – has been rudely shattered since 1979. Although the historical record shows that such a picture is something of an over-simplification, the 1980s have seen profound changes, with far reaching consequences for the role and remit of local authorities in public service provision.

In the eyes of some commentators such changes represent a deliberate attempt to destabilize, and bring about the ultimate demise of local government as presently conceived (Simon 1988). As far as social welfare provision is concerned, local authorities would, according to this scenario end up presiding over a rag-bag of residualized services targeted on a new underclass. For others the end point would be a re-modelled, slimmed-down, more efficient, credible and consumer-orientated system of local government, performing an enabling and facilitative role within a broad-based mixed economy system of welfare.

It is to the analysis of recent changes in public service provision, and their consequences for local government, that this chapter is directed. We describe some of the details of the changes that have taken place and use this sketch as a point of reference for an analysis of the politics of the changes.

It is impossible to base our discussion on an inclusive analysis of all the social services for which local government has a responsibility

Fortunately, comprehensive coverage is not necessary for our purpose. Our interest is not in the substance of policy change *per se*, but what such changes tell us about the present workings and future prospects for local government – its functions, accountabilities and governance.

The service areas upon which we base our discussion – education, housing, and personal social services – were not difficult to select. They are by any definition important areas of governmental responsibility in terms of manpower, budgets, and the impact that the nature and organization of their services can have on the quality of life of people in a local authority's catchment area. Moreover their selection provides us with a cross section of services in terms of different patterns of public-private mix (Papadakis and Taylor-Gooby 1988).

Social welfare needs are met through four overlapping systems; the market, voluntary organizations and agencies, informal networks of families, friends, and neighbours, and the state (Wolfenden 1978). For school-age children, formal education provision is provided overwhelmingly by the state. There is a small, but growing, commercial sector (9 per cent of children) and the remnants of a voluntary sector, but the bulk of children attend state funded, local authority administered schools. At the opposite end of the spectrum personal social service needs are overwhelmingly met through non-state channels, most significantly through family support systems, but also through the market and voluntary agencies. Local authority personal social services departments provide a 'residual' safety-net service to meet needs that are not accommodated through these other systems. Housing occupies an intermediate position, with large numbers of households purchasing their homes through the market (over 65 per cent are owner-occupiers) but with substantial numbers (currently 24 per cent of households) renting publicly-owned stock. A small but growing number of households, rely on voluntary sector provision. In basing our analysis on a discussion of education, housing, and personal social services we are thus able to draw from examples of services that occupy different positions within the 'mixed economy' of welfare.

Finally, the three areas selected have, of course, been the subject of sustained debate and action by central government over the past ten years. Housing was high on the political agenda during the first Thatcher administration (with council house sales and the control of public expenditure on municipal housing becoming key issues) and has returned as a major concern with the 1988 Housing Act. The second and third terms have seen education take centre stage, most recently with the Education Reform Act giving statutory backing to a national curriculum, to 'open rolls' and to the opportunity for parents to vote for their child's school to move from local authority control into a semi-independent, grant-aid status. The personal social services have

79

remained a continuing concern during the Thatcher years, a majo
preoccupation being the attempt to make a reality of 'community-care
policies within a wider context of significant changes in demographi(
patterns (particularly the increase in the proportion of old people) and ;
concerted drive to empty many of the long-stay residentia
establishments for the mentally ill, the mentally handicapped and othe
groups.

We begin this chapter, then, by highlighting a number of genera
trends in local authority welfare provision manifest over the past te)
years, and then exemplify these changes through an overview o
developments in our three chosen areas. Next we focus down on thre(
particular initiatives; the Education Reform Act 1988, the Housing Ac
1988, and Griffith's 1988 proposals for the personal social services
using these to further our examination of current policy and, mor(
particularly, to analyse the politics informing these measures. Finally
we examine such policies and politics with a view to discerning thei
implications for the future of local government.

The Thatcherite challenge; some general themes

All three Thatcher administrations have sustained a high level of interes
and activity in social policy innovation and legislation. Since 1979 th(
government has been at once pro-active, vigorous and interventionis
(Kogan 1987; Malpass and Murie 1987) relying on comfortabl(
parliamentary majorities to enact a wide ranging and radical legislativ(
programme. Reform of key aspects of the social welfare system fo
which local government has major responsibility has, during the thir(
Thatcher term, assumed an explicit and self-consciously 'flagship
status.

At first sight this high profile interventionist stance may appea
strange, emanating as it does from a government with an avowed inten
to 'roll-back' the frontiers of the state. But there is no real contradictio)
here, at least in terms of political ideology: reducing the scope an(
reforming the remit of local social service provision in order to cur)
bureaucracy and extend market freedom requires legislative action
Indeed leading New Right thinkers see a primary function of th
minimalist state as protecting the freedoms of the individual, includin;
their freedom from the arbitrary power of public authorities (Haye)
1960). Cutting back and redefining the role of council housing
extending parental choice and control of the school system, promotin;
family responsibility and voluntary action in meeting welfare needs, ar(
all perfectly consistent with such a philosophy.

Opponents of such policies, of course, see things differently
Increased market choice for the few has been won at the expense of ;

lowered level of public service and a significant diminution of local political choice for the many. Moreover much government action (e.g. the move to a national curriculum in secondary schools) seems straight forwardly centralist and directive in its thrust. In short it would appear to government critics that rather than protecting and enhancing individual freedoms whilst curbing and rationalizing state powers, innovations from the centre have in fact served particularistic interests whilst increasing central control at the expense of local democracy. We shall return to these issues later on.

Moving to the substance of policy change over the past decade a fairly consistent pattern is again discernible. First, it must be noted that reform has, for the most part, been driven by financial and governance considerations. From the 1975 White Paper 'The Attack on Inflation' onwards (see Chapter 4), governments have given priority to the goal of reducing inflation as a central plank in their economic policy. Reductions in public expenditure on social provision is identified as a prime target, both because government borrowing to finance such services increases the money supply (and is thus inflationary) and because public sector growth 'crowds out' the expansion of the wealth creating and growth sustaining private sector. With a few notable exceptions economic goals have become a main determinant of social policy reforms. Substantive service goals – housing production targets, numbers of teachers employed, levels of domiciliary support services – have been overtaken by a primary concern to control expenditure in a situation of reduced finance for services.

The goal of de-municipalizing key aspects of social service provision mirrors and complements these public expenditure concerns. Privatization in its various guises is not only seen, as noted above, to reduce bureaucratic oppressiveness, but also to increase efficiency in the allocation of resources, and to facilitate the growth of social service systems more in tune with the precepts and assumptions of an individualistic psychology and model of human nature. This latter point leads us to note the value dimension within the Thatcherite policy paradigm; self-reliance and the enterprise culture are undermined by high levels of public spending and provision, creating in people an enervating and damaging dependency. To set people free to save, organize, and plan for their own welfare must be the goal, with a minimal and residual safety net of provision available for those who for one reason or another are unable to do this.

Many local authorities, and particularly Labour local authorities have of course rejected these ideas and strongly resisted their policy consequences (Blunkett and Jackson 1987). Whitehall has often encountered difficulties in securing the cooperation of local authorities in implementing new policy priorities and central government has, in consequence, been driven to deploy a variety of strategies to secure the realization of its policies. Three in particular deserve mention; first, new central controls have been introduced, and many existing controls have been more tightly drawn, in order to curb and restructure local authorities' areas of discretion. Second, extensive use has been made of qualgos and quangos, to exercise on central governments behalf some leverage over local authority decision-making. Third, there have been notable examples of direct funding, and increases in central control of provision by central government. Examples of these strategies will be given in ensuing sections.

It is the multiple impact of these changes – in policy content itself, and the means used to secure policy implementation – that has brought discord and conflict to central–local government relations and led to the view that we may be witnessing the demise of traditional forms of local government and local democracy. We shall return to these general issues later, after illustrating the themes identified here through an examination of our three chosen areas of local authority social service provision.

Thatcherism and social policy 1979–89: education, housing and the personal social services

School age education

The established post-war framework for the administration of compulsory school age education has come under sustained pressure for change since 1979, as central government's education policies, driven by financial and governance imperatives, have generated a consistent bias towards centralization. True, there has also been some concern to reform the content of the schools' curriculum, but this has also been driven by wider economic considerations – concerned with how schools can better serve the goal of generating a more profitable and competitive economy.

The steep post-war increase in public expenditure on education began to level off during the 1970s and with the Conservatives return to power in 1979 it ceased. Since then, whether or not education has sustained the cut-backs and borne the brunt of the government's economic measures to the same extent as some other services is debatable, and has been addressed in the previous chapter. Certainly local education authorities (LEAs), headteachers, and school governors have experienced difficulties that have been attributed to underfunding; for example, in the purchase of books and equipment, in the ability of many schools to sustain a broad-based curriculum, and in the difficulties encountered in maintaining teacher morale and commitment.

Interpretations of expenditure trends are made difficult because, whilst on the one hand cash availability has increased and is reflected in an average overall increase in money spent per pupil, on the other hand a large proportion of such increases has been taken up in salary increases and other costs which are not necessarily reflected in direct qualitative improvements in services provided to pupils (Kogan 1987).

Financial tensions and constraints have been buttressed by a series of legislative changes that have served to further constrain the freedom of manoeuvre, or lay new prescriptive duties upon LEAs. The sum total of both these sets of changes has been one of increasing central control of education at the expense of local discretion. Some examples may be given: a system of education support grants have been introduced, the funding for which (nearly £100m in 1986–7) is deducted from the general rate support grant; LEAs must obtain DES approval for project expenditure. Again, in-service training for teachers is now subject to central control; LEAs must develop their training plans in accordance with centrally determined criteria if they are to receive grants from the £200m that is allocated from the centre for such purposes.

The bias of legislative provision – in Education Acts that reached the statute book in 1980, 1981, and 1986 – has also served to weaken the LEAs control over the running of local schools. For example, changes in the membership and powers of governing bodies have served to shift the balance of power from LEAs to governors. It is now mandatory for children with special needs to be educated in 'ordinary' schools. All parents now have the right of appeal against LEA's decisions about the placement of their children; the Secretary of State for Education can now take powers to make regulations for the appraisal of teachers; and all sorts of duties are now laid on LEAs with respect to the way that aspects of the curriculum (e.g. political and sex education) is undertaken. It can also be noted that the rights of LEAs and teachers to engage in free collective bargaining has been removed.

Perhaps more significant in its impact than these direct efforts at centralization has been the development and use of the Manpower Services Commission (renamed the Training Commission in 1988) as a primary instrument for achieving indirect leverage over LEAs. The Training and Vocational Education Initiative (TVEI) provides an instructive example of how this non-elected commission has become an effective tool in central government's bid to achieve policy control of the practices of LEAs. The TVEI was launched in 1982, designed to secure a more technical and vocational education for 14–19 year olds in schools and colleges and has now expanded to the extent that the vast majority of local authorities are involved in submitting schemes to the Training Commission for a slice of the £90m funding available. Views differ about the educational value of the programme, but few LEAs have been happy about the lack of consultation over its development and the way that this quite major attempt at curriculum change has cast them in the role of non-executant agent of a centrally-controlled quango.

This and similar types of scheme promoted by the Training Commission (CPVE, YTS, etc) deserve attention for two further reasons; first they demonstrate a concern by government to influence (or, as we shall see later, prescribe) the content of the school curriculum – a development that dates back to the mid-1970s but which has gathered momentum since 1979. Second, they illustrate the drive towards vocationalism, a movement underlined by the 1986 launch of a plan to set up a series of city technology colleges directly funded by central government and private enterprise, and intended to provide gifted inner-city children with a vocational and technical education. Perhaps more symbolic than anything else – only a limited number are planned and they have been slow to get off the ground – they do nevertheless provide a further illustration of central government's willingness to by-pass LEAs as one strategy in their attempt to direct educational policy change.

Housing

Since the end of the First World War housing needs in Britain have been met through a mixture of private, public, and voluntary sector provision. The balance of provision by each of these sectors has varied over time: private owner-occupation has steadily increased (such that many, on both left and right of the political spectrum, now regard home ownership as the 'natural' choice of most households), while private renting has dwindled to a numerically minute sector even smaller than the voluntary (housing association) sector. Publicly-owned and managed (council) housing grew rapidly after each world war but over the last 40 years the proportion of people housed in this sector has gradually declined such that some expert commentators, after reviewing long-term changes in the British housing system, talk of a 100 year restructuring process, from a largely privately-rented, to a largely privately-owned system (Malpas and Murie 1987).

Certainly the Conservative's housing policy since 1979 has, for the most part, served to accentuate and accelerate these trends. Mr Thatcher's first administration was brought to power pledging to expand owner-occupation and stimulate the revival of the private market for rented properties, sell council houses to sitting tenants, and by ensuring that public resources were targeted on those who were unable to help themselves, reinforce the trend towards seeing public housing as 'welfare housing'. These policies were, of course, predicated on the perceived need to vigorously cut back public expenditure in all of the social services administered by local government. Housing has been the area to most seriously experience the brunt of the Government's expenditure policies. As chapter 4 shows housing's share of public expenditure nearly halved between 1979 and 1988. Housing also illustrates another of the general trends noted previously. Driven by concerns about expenditure and ownership, Conservative concerns have been directed almost exclusively to tenure policy. There has been little effort to address traditional areas of housing concern like the number of houses built, or to set targets for renovation and improvement of the stock, or to secure a reduction in the number of homeless people.

The goal of de-municipalizing significant amounts of public housing has led to a reduced role for local authorities within this area of social provision. There are now over one million fewer housing units administered by local authorities than there were in 1979.

Second, the government's chosen instruments to achieve policy change has, as in education, served to reduce local discretion and increase central scrutiny and control. The 'right-to-buy' legislation has been a case in point; it prescribed in great detail how the act was to be implemented. Changes in housing benefits had a similar effect. The 1982 Social Security and Housing Benefit Act, which unified housing assistance (rent and rate rebate allowances and supplementary benefit rent assistance were replaced by one overall housing allowance), shifted control by removing major parts of the scheme from local authority administration to the central government social security administration. Along with the declining role of local housing authorities has gone an enhanced role for a major quango: the Housing Corporation. More public money is now channelled through this body, to fund the activities of housing associations. The latter have now become a significant provider of publicly-funded housing and carry out a very substantial amount of improvement and rehabilitation work. One clear advantage for central government of channelling public money through the Housing Corporation is that this body is much more easily bent to their will than are the local authorities. This represents another example of the general strategy of by-passing the local authorities.

Finally it should be noted that apart from encouraging the privatization of council houses, the government has taken a number of other measures to support and strengthen the private housing market. One outcome of relevance has been the more pro-active role of the building societies and their self-promotion as a 'partner' in pursuing government housing policy (Building Societies Association 1984). Societies have made special arrangements to facilitate the funding of council house sales and have taken over from local authorities the role of major mortgage suppliers for older properties (Murie 1987). It may be noted that the 1986 Building Societies Act now enables larger societies to build, own, and provide houses for rent and in at least one instance a major building society has been involved in taking over, improving, and managing a large estate on behalf of a local authority (Stoker 1985).

Personal social services and community care

Of the three areas of social provision examined here the personal social services are most clearly operating within a 'mixed economy' of welfare. Provision of social and community care for the elderly, the disabled, the mentally ill, and the mentally handicapped and for children and others at risk, is the responsibility of local authorities in conjunction with expanding voluntary and private sectors. Although it must always be remembered that 'informal' agencies of care – family, friends, and neighbours – still remain the largest and most significant providers.

Not only is the fact of a mixed system self-evident, but there is also substantial professional consensus and party-political agreement that the personal social services system should embrace, and build upon, a plural pattern of provision with care 'interwoven' from a range of sources. In a way, then, the system represents a kind of paradigm case for a Thatcherite–Conservative model of local service provision and prompts the question, in such a model what is the remit of a local authority department responsible for social care provision? Two views predominate. They are not necessarily mutually exclusive, although it seems that the second one is currently in the ascendant within government circles. The first view holds that the local authority personal social services department should function as an instrument of last resort, a back-stop form of provision to be called upon when other systems (family and friends, the market) have failed. For a time during the first Thatcher administration, Patrick Jenkin, then Secretary of State, advocated such a residual role, going as far as to argue that 'the informal sector lies at the centre with statutory services and the organised voluntary sector providing back up, expertise and support' (quoted in Webb and Wistow 1987). His successor was more inclined to place the local authority service centre-stage, not in the sense of being required to take responsibility for meeting all need, but in the sense of performing a strategic role in planning and orchestrating the various components in the mixed economy of welfare provision. As noted, it is this latter view that currently attracts most support. Local authority social services are seen as partners in community care, with a particular responsibility to coordinate and integrate the different need-meeting systems within an overall planning framework. It should be noted that the emphasis is on community care, a concept with a wide variety of meaning (see Walker 1982; Bulmer 1987).

So, how have things worked out in practice since 1979? In the first place, expenditure controls have prevented local authorities from responding to demands from their local communities. Government has recognized an exceptional growth in need for community care resources – need brought about by, for example, the growth in the number of elderly people, the cost implications of new legislation like the 1983 Mental Health Act, the emergence of new needs (drug abuse, AIDS), and the impact of long-term unemployment. As a consequence a 2 per cent per annum growth allowance has been allocated during most of this government's years in office. However two things have happened; costs have tended to rise more quickly in the personal social services than elsewhere, so a 2 per cent annual increase does little more than ensure that existing levels of provision do not deteriorate. Second, the operation of DHSS discretionary payments has been allowed to underwrite residential care provision in a way that militates against community care. Local authority personal social services departments have been able, to some extent, to shift resources from residential to community support, but only because the private sector, supported by rocketing social security payments has fuelled the consolidation of residential provision.

This conclusion illustrates a more general point, that there has been a lack of integrated planning for community care in Whitehall (Wistow 1987). Not only are the unintended consequences of income support policies undermining community care policies, but there are other discontinuities and contradictions too. Responsibilities between health authorities and personal social services departments are fragmented, as witnessed in the 'silting up' of joint finance arrangements, and there has been an absence of strategic planning in the running down of the long-stay institutions. Finally we must note the point made by Walker that community care policy seems to be promoted without any clear idea concerning the most appropriate 'mix' of provision in geographical areas that experience different patterns of need, social and family structure and so on (Walker 1987).

If the personal social services do represent a 'paradigm case' of government policy – of a local authority department both orchestrating and making a contribution to a mixed system of welfare – than it would seem that much more 'orchestrating' (not to mention 'contribution') is necessary from Whitehall too. Whether or not government has the will to do this, given its free market dispositions remains a moot point. Without both, the personal social services are destined to become an even more residual service.

The politics of social policy

An overview of trends in a particular policy area only takes us so far; a more rounded picture of the future of local government service provision demands an examination of the politics that inform those trends. This is best approached by an examination of particular policy proposals. 'Politics' is here used in the sense outlined in the introduction to this book, and recent proposals in the fields of education, housing and personal social services are chosen for examination in terms of those dimensions. Such an approach enables judgements to be made about the respective merits of three contested interpretations of the Thatcherite project for local public service provision.

The first of these interpretations suggests that central government plans for social services are best summed up as an exercise in 'One Nation Statecraft'. In this view the task of government is to deploy (the often limited) steerage capacity that is available to state agencies to pursue policies which are, as far as possible, in the interests of all. Following the 'New Conservatism' of the years following the Second World War and of the traditions of Disraelian 'One Nation' Conservatism (O'Gorman 1986), this perspective recognizes a role for the state as an agency of reform, and as a facilitator of economic and social regeneration, albeit on a modest scale and in a pragmatic style. The ability of government to effectively plan any area of societal activity is, of course, severely limited; many policy initiatives are of necessity driven by exogenous factors such as demographic pressure (e.g. in the social services), the need for public expenditure constraint (e.g. in housing) and the need for economic modernization and the restructuring of labour markets (through education). Nevertheless the scope and responsibility to work for change is a duty of government.

The second view suggests that the Conservative Government's carefully constructed imagery be taken more or less at face value. A decade of reforms in local public service provision have resulted, it is said, from the focused pursuit of New Right values, conviction politics and firm political leadership. Here the themes we have already touched upon – the trends to centralization, residualization and privatization – are interpreted as part of a self-conscious project to re-balance the role of state and market in society, and restore a proper balance between individual freedom and collective responsibility (Green 1987).

Or a third interpretation is possible: that in seeking to make sense of recent changes it is necessary to look no further than interest groups and wider, 'class' politics. The critique of state bureaucracy, the elevation of consumer choice, the promotion of the market within a 'mixed economy' of welfare, and all the other ingredients of New Right ideology are seen as just that – an ideological cover for the advancement of particularistic interests like private landlordism and property finance agencies, private education, and commercial nursing and residential homes.

School reform and the Education Act 1988

At first sight the education reforms introduced in 1988 do appear to confirm a break with post-war attempts to create 'one nation' through education. It has been predicted that the reforms will prove fatally divisive, for example by allowing (eventually encouraging) schools to opt out of LEA control, thereby opening the door to the reintroduction of selectivity, with consequent feelings of rejection and alienation amongst the system's failures. For, despite the progressive introduction of comprehensive schooling, children from middle-class backgrounds have continued to benefit from the present educational system. On the face of it this makes it difficult to understand why the government should seek wholesale reform. Why should a Thatcherite Government break with policies that seem to carry electoral pitfalls for the party?

Two answers seems to flow from this question. The first is the argument that recent reforms affirm the ascendancy of fundamentalist New Right thinking in educational policy-making. The opportunities for schools to opt out of local authority control and into a grant-maintained status, enhanced parental choice, devolved budgets, recording children's attainment on standardized tests at regular intervals, and publicizing school performance indicators – all of these measures are congruent with the promotion of a radical, market-based orientation to schools and schooling. Such reforms help to ensure that only those schools that remain responsive to consumer demand will survive. 'Needs', as defined by educational producers (the teachers, the educational planners, advisors and administrators) are to take second place. Whether in reality parents will have more, or less, of a voice is open to question. It may be further noted that alongside the emphasis on choice, markets and consumerism, goes the other element of New Right thinking identified by Hall (1983) as 'authoritarian populism'. The curriculum reforms represent a return to a more balanced and traditional curriculum, one that will rein in the wilder excesses of woolly-minded progressives, and appeal to the silent majority of middle England. Certainly, it has been suggested that individual schools could well find their room to manoeuvre minimized by a concentration of central government powers and of weakening countervailing local authority influence. Be that as it may, the public and explicit justification for the reforms seems to remain firmly grounded in New Right thinking.

The second answer suggests pragmatism and continuity; that the government has been concerned to respond to the disquiet and unease about state education increasingly voiced from a variety of quarters. It has, in other words, been seeking a new national consensus about the direction and focus of educational provision for the next quarter century. Parental disquiet has been one of those pressures – an unease that was increasingly voiced in the early 1970s, and that was recognized by the Callaghan Government in the later 1970s. The Callaghan speech at Ruskin College in 1976 was designed to open a 'great educational debate'. Parental unhappiness with the content of the school curriculum, with the way their children were being taught, and with the lack of preparation their children were being given for entry into employment were to be part of that debate (Hopkins 1979). Employers, too, were unhappy about the educational status quo; schools seemed unable to harness children's technical abilities and school leavers were ill-prepared for entry into the world of work. These themes were taken up by Sir Keith Joseph when he was Minister of Education. He believed that the educational status quo was indefensible; it created two nations through its advancement of the 'academic' and able pupils at the expense of the majority, and second, the general thrust of the curriculum marginalized the technological, an area of the curriculum increasingly central to the needs of the UK economy as it moved towards the twenty-first century. It was the teachers and self-serving 'producer' interests which, in this view, offered the most reactionary resistance to such reforms and it was their resistance which prompted the government to use external bodies like the MSC to apply some of the leverage necessary to secure change. The 1988 Act thus represents a further injection of measures necessary to reform the educational system to the benefit of all.

Both of these answers carry some element of truth. Yet neither answer is fully satisfying, principally because they cannot make sense of the various anomalies and contradictions contained within the educational reforms. For example the attempt to move towards a quasi-market approach seems to be belied by the increasingly centralist and prescriptive approach to the core curriculum, pupil testing, and policy control. The act is seen as promoting parental choice but at the same time the exercise of that choice might be minimized with schools opting out. Again most of the reforms relate to state-supported schools; if reform is predicated on 'one nation' and economic arguments then why are the public schools exempt? Surely this is both socially divisive and, in view of what is known about the elite opportunities open to those with a public school education, hardly a reassurance that future social leadership will have the technological expertise that industry is supposed to require for competitive survival.

At least some of these contradictions are dissolved if we turn to a third answer. This explanation suggests that the Education Act is in essence a straightforwardly Conservative measure – a highly partisan set of reforms directed at satisfying the interests of Conservative supporters and ensuring that education better serves the needs of industry and commerce. At the same time the measures seek to check the power of Labour education authorities. A particular target here are the so-called 'looney-left' authorities which take to extreme their concerns with anti-racist and anti-sexist education, promote non-traditional family structures, and sanction 'unbalanced' consideration of things like peace studies.

But the appeal is not just to those middle-class parents 'trapped' within Brent or other inner-city bastions of 'extremism'; it also represents an attempt to strengthen, across the country, traditional educational values and to dilute the 'progressivism' of professional interests. A national curriculum and regular testing, along with the devolution of power away from the local authority producer interests, to governing bodies with enhanced parental and business representation, can be used to secure a more 'formal' curriculum, one concerned with instilling objective knowledge in a structured and disciplined atmosphere which prepares young people for the instrumental and competitive world of work.

The evolving needs of industry, for a workforce that is able to cope with new technology, can also be accommodated – through periodic central adjustments to the core curriculum, and through the leverage of government-controlled funding in special support grants. Finally, middle-class parental values are further safeguarded through the open-rolls provision and the right of a school, on the basis of a majority vote by parents, to 'opt' into independent grant-maintained status. This latter possibility is attractive for two reasons. In the first place it offers the possibility of a revival of the old grammar school regime much beloved by those middle-class parents who could not afford to pay the fees demanded by the public schools. And in the second place the door is opened to possible eventual privatization of large parts of the school system.

The politics of housing and community care

We have focused on the politics of recent educational reform in some depth for two reasons. The discussion has enabled us to flesh out a number of general lines of argument, that can with little difficulty, be applied to the other two areas of policy change that have preoccupied us in this chapter. Second, because education is a service dominated (currently!) by state provision, these arguments – and particularly the ones concerned to distinguish between New Right and One Nation thinking – are thrown into sharp relief. Although the greater dominance

91

of private sector provision in housing and personal social services renders the rationale for contemporary reform of the state sector in these areas of provision less stark, the distinctions drawn between the three interpretations of the politics behind such changes hold good.

Thus, we can see that policies for both local authority housing and community care provision continue to be promoted and justified on the basis of New Right assumptions and values. The White Paper preceding the 1988 Housing Act (HMSO 1987) advanced arguments about the importance of markets and consumer choice in the effective and efficient meeting of housing needs. Local authority provision came in for the usual battery of market-liberal criticisms – that its administration was insensitive to tenant needs and that it was inefficient and wasteful in its use of resources. Estates were too often badly managed, tenants were alienated and housing subsidies were indiscriminately targeted. The answer to these deficiencies lies in better management. But improvement will not be achieved by exhortation alone; it will come through the creation of more balanced, more 'mixed' estates. This is something that can be achieved through the opportunities the legislation gives to tenants to enjoy a greater choice of tenure – private ownership, housing association, and housing co-operative. Here is the same critique of, and challenge to, the local authority as 'provider' that we saw in the discussion of education. The theme is taken up again in the report prepared for the government by Sir Roy Griffiths (1988) on community care. As in housing, so in community care, the role of the local authority is to ensure that the needs of the elderly, the mentally ill and the handicapped are assessed and met, but not necessarily by direct provision. The ideal is the mixed economy of welfare, with choice and competition in provision provided by the mechanism of the market. Underpinning the philosophy, is, once more, an explicit recognition of the role of the family as the appropriate front-line resource in times of member need.

On the other hand, many of the reforms are interpretable within what we have called the One Nation Statecraft interpretation. Thus the sectoral changes in housing, it is maintained, continue to demonstrate the 'naturalness' of private home ownership, that this form of tenure above all other, constitutes the overwhelming preference for most of the British people. Similarly, most people, it is argued, value independent living, and when frailty or disability begins to threaten that independence, look to a state system of community care that acts as support and guarantor of continued independence for as long as possible. Housing and community care policies are in this view both recognizing, and contributing to, established national preferences and values.

These two interpretations are, it is clear, mutually reinforcing in many ways, but once again it is all to easy to expose anomalies and contradictions in such apparently straightforward scenarios. The preference for private home ownership might look rather less 'natural' if the housing market was, in fact, left to operate freely and without exchequer 'subsidy' of mortgage tax relief and windfall exemptions from capital gains (current costs of £4.8bn on mortgage tax relief and £2.5bn on capital gains). The first of these two gains to home owners costs the exchequer more, and it can be argued is far more 'indiscriminate' than the subsidies and allowances that accrue to public sector tenants. It should also be noted that despite the success of the governments 'right to buy' legislation, the majority of public sector tenants have made a positive choice to remain in their council houses, turning aside from the combined attraction of large discounts and the windfall gains that home ownership brings in a time of inflating house prices.

As far as community care is concerned there is evidence that everyday assumptions about mutuality and reciprocity in family life, along with assumptions about the normalcy of locally proximate, three-generation family structures, warrant careful scrutiny and evaluation if they are to underpin policy prescriptions in any realistic way (Bulmer 1987). Demographic and social changes are having a significant impact on the social structure and normative expectations of many family members and these often seem at odds with the more simplistic 'familistic' values that are used in the rhetoric of community care. Questions of income levels and material standards of living are also important in understanding how community care is viewed in concrete situations, by carers and cared-for alike. Finally the significant gender biases implicit in many approaches to community care must not be overlooked – carers are often women.

So, as in consideration of the politics of education, a rounded view of the politics of housing and of community care prompts the deployment of the third – interest groups – perspective. Political support for such policies is clearly not unrelated to income, and other material and class related factors. And it must not be overlooked that a growing army of people make a living from the construction, finance, and exchange of private housing and that these same groups have a not unrelated interest in the private 'packaging' of community care.

Conclusions

The overview of policy developments in the fields of education, housing and personal social services that was presented in the first part of this chapter led to an identification of a a number of paradoxes and contradictions. The Thatcher administrations have, at one and the same time been pro-active and prescriptive while also seeking to 'roll back' the frontiers of the state. A whole battery of new measures and agencies have been used to increase central policy direction and control over local government while, at the same time, the rhetoric has involved an appeal to expanded consumer choice; to curbing and rationalizing state power.

The discussion in the second half of the chapter has enabled us to dissolve some of these contradictions. In terms of the politics of recent social policy change, doctrinal New Right values and pragmatic One Nation perspectives have been used, in tandem, to promote and sustain apparently diverse and contrary policy tendencies. The demonstrable appeal to middle class and other traditional Conservative interests, has, we have further argued provided the linkage that keeps these two potentially antagonistic political value systems, coupled together. The strength of contemporary Thatcherism resides in the ability to appeal to all three of these sustaining philosophies.

Such a picture, if drawn correctly, would appear to offer little immediate scope for local government to offer an effective challenge to its future as prescribed from the Thatcherite centre. There is a self-reinforcing coherence, at the ideological and pragmatic levels, about the future role and remit of local government service provision in Britain that has not, so far, evoked an equally coherent and sustained ideological and material challenge from opposition forces.

References

Building Societies Association (1984) *New Legislation for Building Societies*, London.

Bulmer, M. (1987) *The Social Basis of Community Care*, London: Allen & Unwin.

Blunkett, D. and Jackson, K. (1987) *Democracy in Crisis: Town Halls Respond*, London: Hogarth.

Dunleavy, P. and Rhodes, R.A.W. (1986) 'Government Beyond Whitehall', in H. Drucker, P. Dunleavy, A. Gamble, and G. Peele (eds) *Developments in British Politics*, London: Macmillan.

Green, D.G. (1987) *The New Right*, London: Wheatsheaf Books.

Griffiths, Sir F. (1988) *Community Care: Agenda for Action*, London: HMSO.

Hayek, F. (1960) *The Constitution of Liberty*, London: Routledge & Kegan Paul.

HMSO (1987) *Housing: The Government's Proposals*, Cm 214, London.

Hopkins, A. (1979) *The School Debate*, Harmondsworth: Penguin Books.

Kogan, M. (1987) 'Education', in M. Parkinson *Reshaping Local Government*, Oxford: Policy Journals.

Lawton, D. (1980) *The Politics of the School Curriculum*, London: Routledge & Kegan Paul.

Malpass, P.L. and Murie, A. (1987) *Housing Policy and Practice*, Basingstoke: Macmillan.
Murie, A. (1987) 'Housing', in M. Parkinson *Reshaping Local Government*, Oxford: Policy Journals.
O'Gorman, F. (1986) *British Conservatism*, London: Longmans.
Papadakis, E. and Taylor-Gooby, P. (1987) *The Private Provision of Public Welfare*, Brighton: Wheatsheaf Books.
Simon, B. (1988) *Bending the Rules: The Baker 'Reform' of Education*, London: Lawrence & Wishart.
Stoker, G. (1985) 'The Building Societies and the Conservatives, Housing Strategy into the late 1980s; *Critical Social Policy*, 12 (Spring).
Walker, A. (ed.) (1982) *Community Care*, Oxford: Basil Blackwell.
Walker, A. (1987) 'Pluralism in the Personal Social Services: Some Guidelines for the Future', in J. Rea Price *et al.* (eds) *The Future Role of Social Service Departments*, London: Policy Studies Institute.
Webb, A. and Wistow, G. (1987) *Social Work, Social Care and Social Planning: the Personal Social Services since Seebohm*, London: Longman.
Wolfenden, J. (1978) *The Future of Voluntary Organizations*, London: Croom Helm.

Chapter six

Local economic development

Introduction

Economic development is both a relatively new and highly contentious function of local authorities. It is at the centre of the whole debate over the future role and activities of elected local institutions in the altered political environment associated with the advent of Thatcherism.

The novelty of the economic development function may perhaps be questioned. Some of the policy initiatives now being utilized have some precedents in the inter-war period (Chandler and Lawless 1985). They are, however, new in the context of the post-war period. More fundamentally it is of course true that local government has always and inevitably had a major impact on local economies. The local council is often the largest employer in the area and both its capital and current expenditure have massive implications for local economic activity, both directly and indirectly. Yet in the past this impact on the local economy was essentially not only unplanned but scarcely even considered. It was the casual by-product of the pursuit of other policies – in housing, education, social services, and other mainstream services – rather than a central policy objective in itself. This is no longer the case. The proliferation of Departments of Industry and Economic Development, of similarly titled committees, of employment units, and new official posts involving economic development responsibilities is some indication of the new climate.

Local government's rather belated but not unnatural interest in local economic development has been paralleled, perhaps rather more surprisingly, by a reorientation of central government economic development policies towards intervention in fairly narrowly-defined local areas. Before the election of the Thatcher Government in 1979, this central and local state involvement in local economic development was essentially collaborative and mutually reinforcing. Since 1979 the relationship, while retaining some elements of partnership, has become increasingly competitive.

Thus while the novelty of the function might perhaps be questioned, its controversial nature is only too clear. At an ideological level, the whole role and scope of the public sector in economic development is sharply contested. Some free market purists would reject the need for any state intervention in the local economy, arguing that it inevitably distorts optimum resource allocation and involves some loss of efficiency. Such a purist approach may sometimes appear in the rhetoric of the Thatcher Government, but scarcely in its practice, for the Thatcher administration has become involved in a wide range of interventionist initiatives in the area of local economic development. The real battle has not been over the case for intervention, but over how that intervention should be managed, and, more specifically, who should be responsible for it.

This chapter will seek first to explain the relatively new interest in (both local and central) state economic intervention at local level. The ideological implications of the advent of the Thatcher Government for local economic strategies are then discussed in broad terms. The approaches of local government to economic development and the contrasting initiatives of central government in economic regeneration at the local level are reviewed in rather more detail in two further sections. A concluding section examines the politics of implementation and the nature of the challenge of Thatcherism to local government's role in economic development.

The shift towards local economic strategies

The new emphasis on economic intervention at the local level was the product of two, initially distinct, policy problems identified by politicians, civil servants and academics in the late 1960s and early 1970s. On the one hand there was the growing preoccupation from 1968 onwards with the problems of Britain's inner cities. On the other hand there was a worsening economic crisis, coupled with an apparent failure of traditional policy remedies.

What came to be identified as 'the inner-city problem' was not at first seen as essentially an economic problem (McKay and Cox 1979). It was forcibly brought to the notice of politicians through riots and disturbances, but was also emphasized in a series of official and semi-official reports (Plowden, DoE Inner Area Studies, Scarman Report, etc). Professionals, academics, and politicians all tended to redefine the nature of the problem in terms of their own service, discipline, or ideology. Thus 'the problem' was seen in terms of race relations, inadequate educational facilities, poor housing, bad planning, inappropriate policing, deficient community facilities, and unsatisfactory social services. A common assumption underlying many initial policy responses was that personal and familial inadequacies lay at the heart of the problem (Lawless 1981: 6).

Nursery schools and play facilities in inner-city areas would remedy the alleged deficiencies in upbringing. Community social workers would stimulate self-help initiatives. Environmental schemes would help transform neighbourhoods and, hopefully, attitudes. A measure of positive discrimination would help break into the cycle of deprivation, and prevent one generation from passing on its inadequacies to the next.

The perception of the problem changed with the experience of policy failure and research. A common finding of the ill-fated Community Development Projects was that the problems in their areas reflected structural changes in the economy outside the control of the local community. The Inner Area Studies reached similar conclusions (see Mckay and Cox 1979 for a summary). Peter Shore's 1977 White Paper (Cmnd 6845) marked a sea-change in official thinking. The inner-city problem was now perceived as essentially an economic problem. Poverty and other associated characteristics of Britain's inner urban areas were seen as symptoms of unemployment and low pay, which were in turn related to low levels of economic activity. It became axiomatic that the regeneration of the inner cities depended on the regeneration of economic activity. This in turn reflected a major reversal of previous national policy, which had sought to redirect economic activity away from the older industrial centres.

By the late 1970s the national economic recession had deepened the problems of the older urban areas. It is important to recall that when the Urban Programme was launched in 1968, unemployment was still well below a million. It was possible then to view the inner cities as islands of poverty in a general sea of prosperity. Problems could be seen in terms of particular characteristics of the areas – high concentrations of ethnic minorities, old schools, above average numbers of large families and one parent families, neglected older housing or unsatisfactory high-rise flats, a depressing environment. Ten years later the inner-city areas could no longer be seen as isolated pockets. They increasingly appeared as extreme manifestations of the general failure of the British economy (Solesbury 1986). This was particularly apparent as areas which had been relatively prosperous in the 1960s, such as the West Midlands and Greater Manchester, experienced high unemployment and its associated problems, which other areas such as Tyneside and Merseyside had known earlier.

Irrespective of their past preoccupations with inner-city problems, local authorities in the larger urban areas would of necessity have had to react to the impact of the national recession on their own areas, if only because of the increased pressures placed on their services by high unemployment and the loss of rate income consequent on business failures. Quite apart from any natural humanitarian concern, the alleviation of unemployment and economic regeneration made good business sense to many local councils.

The time was also ripe for experiments at local level. Traditional national and regional policy tools had been found wanting. The combination of high inflation and high unemployment, 'stagflation', seemed to invalidate what had passed as Keynesian assumptions. A Labour Prime Minister sternly warned that it was no longer possible for the country to spend its way out of recession. Regional policy was also substantially discredited. There was thus a pragmatic case for experimenting with alternative approaches at a different level, involving different agencies. The election of the Thatcher Government in 1979 considerably sharpened the ideological debate over the means to achieve economic regeneration in the older urban areas, however.

The Thatcher Government and local economic strategies

The election of the Thatcher Government did not in one sense lead to any radical change in the perception of inner-city problems. The Church of England's Commission was told by DoE officials 'that the present Government largely accepted the analysis in the 1977 White Paper' (Church of England 1985). The problem was still perceived as essentially an economic one. The prime need was to attract new investment and create more jobs in deprived urban areas. That indicated a need for initiatives at the local area level. Indeed, such local strategies were apparently the only ideologically acceptable solution left to the government. Keynesianism had been abandoned more in sorrow than in anger by the previous Labour Government. It was deliberately repudiated by the monetarists who were dominant in the new Thatcher administration. Regional policy found even less favour, and regional policy instruments have been progressively dismantled (Green 1987). Yet the special problems of the inner cities were acknowledged and the need for some specific policy initiatives was readily conceded by the Conservatives, even before the 1981 riots once again brought the deprived urban areas to the top of the political agenda.

Yet while the Thatcher Government accepted the need for economic regeneration of the older urban areas, sharp ideological differences developed over how such economic regeneration was to be achieved, and who should have the prime responsibility for achieving it (Lawless 1988).

For the left, inner-city decay was a clear example of market failure. Decline could only be reversed by more state intervention and planning (Mackintosh and Wainwright 1987). For the New Right, planning controls, and the high taxation which was the corollary of state

99

intervention, were part of the problem rather than the solution. A preference for free market solutions, for a reliance on the private sector rather than the public sector implied a rejection of local government as an appropriate policy instrument. Local government was perceived by the gurus of the New Right as bureaucratic, inflexible, and tied to the vested interests of its own workforce and traditional clientele. Local government had either created the problem, or at the very least signally failed to solve it. Imbued with such thinking it was scarcely surprising that the Thatcher Government should seek to by-pass local government and use alternative agencies to tackle the problem.

Sweeping gains for the Labour Party in local elections in 1980 and 1981 gave an increasingly partisan flavour to the conflict between central and local government over economic strategy. On the one hand Labour councils, horrified at the impact of monetarist strategies on their own areas, sought to remedy the perceived deficiencies of national policy on unemployment through local initiatives (Mackintosh and Wainwright 1987: 13; Blunkett and Jackson 1987: chapter 6). Faced with a need also to rethink cherished socialist nostrums, some Labour theorists proclaimed the need for a more decentralized, consumer-oriented socialism as opposed to the hitherto prevailing centralized state socialism, associated with post-war Labour governments. Exclusion from power at national level, coupled with a firm hold on all the major industrial cities added to the attraction of 'local socialism' (Boddy 1984; Gyford 1985). Local economic initiatives thus came to be seen as the very essence of socialism.

Already disposed by background and ideological presuppositions to suspicion of local government, Thatcher's Government was faced with something of a counter-offensive from the new urban left. It was never likely that the more radical initiatives launched by some labour councils would be acceptable to a government pledged to restrain the growth of public expenditure and rein back the frontiers of the state. New Right economic theories suggested that such radical initiatives would be positively harmful. Political considerations reinforced economic theory. A Conservative central government could not allow Labour councils the prime role in a major area of policy, nor to claim the credit for any success which might be achieved. Ideology and partisan political interest both pointed towards solutions involving central government in direct partnership with private enterprise. Local economic strategies thus became central to the ideological battleground between the new urban left and the New Right, and economic development policies pursued by Labour councils thus acquired an ideological significance beyond their intrinsic value. They were either seen as the essence of socialism in action, or as models for the next Labour Government to apply at national level. Similarly, new initiatives introduced by the government carried a symbolic significance over and above their contribution to economic regeneration. Geoffrey Howe claimed that if Labour councils could be persuaded to bid for enterprise zones the government would be winning the ideological battle. Thus the election of the Thatcher Government, while it did not involve any sharp shift in the perception of the problem certainly produced a marked polarization in strategies and over responsibility for policy. Local authorities developed a range of initiatives underpinned by various ideological assumptions from mainstream Keynesian to Marxist. Central government devised its own distinctive policy instruments, which largely by-passed local government. It is now necessary to review these two contrasting sets of initiatives in rather more detail.

Approaches to economic development by local authorities

Until the late 1970s, in so far as local authorities pursued conscious economic development strategies at all, the emphasis was on promotional activities to attract inward investment (Chandler and Lawless 1985). Characteristically, advertisements suggested that particular cities were the centres of the universe, the hub of an extensive network of communications, and with all kinds of other natural and acquired advantages for the location of new industrial and commercial activity. The value of such promotional work now tends to be viewed more sceptically. Essentially it is seen as a zero sum game, with local authorities competing against each other for a share of a relatively fixed quantity of new investment. Promotion is unlikely to generate extra employment nationally, only to redistribute employment. Moreover, national and multi-national companies attracted by investment grants and regional employment premiums sometimes subsequently sought to rationalize their operations, and relocate activities in response to new inducements from other governments or other local authorities. Foot-loose industry in pursuit of maximum profits owes no loyalty to specific areas. This was particularly evident to some local councils as the recession began to bite in the 1970s. Indigenous firms often sought to weather the storm, not always successfully. Recently attracted multi-nationals tended to close plant and shed labour.

Economic development initiatives in the 1980s have embraced a variety of specific strategies. Attempts have been made to classify these. Hasluck (1987) describes three different responses to urban unemployment: the neo-classical competitive approach, the structuralist/Keynesian approach and the radical/Marxist approach. Moore (1988) outlines three broadly similar models, which he calls liberal market, modified market, and socialized models of economic policy. Although these are helpful, inevitably they rather oversimplify the diversity encountered in practice.

A few right-wing Conservative authorities have pursued purposive neo-liberal market-oriented strategies. Places like Wandsworth and Southend have provided experimental testing grounds for competitive tendering and privatization. Wandsworth has contracted out fifteen services and reduced its staff from 3,300 to 1,600. The assumption behind such a strategy is that the public sector is a burden on the economy and interferes with the operation of market forces and inhibits enterprise. Contracting out exposes the council's services to competition and provides more opportunities for local business. Lower business rates achieved through cost-cutting exercises reduce the tax burden on private enterprise and aids expansion, while the disposal of the council's housing stock facilitates the free movement of labour. Thus, it is argued, a positive liberal market strategy can stimulate local economic activity and employment.

Surprisingly perhaps, in view of the dominance of liberal-market rhetoric, such a purist approach has been relatively uncommon. Significantly, the authorities most publicly associated with a market strategy are in the south, where unemployment and other associated problems are less acute. Commonly, even when cities in the north and midlands have been Conservative-controlled, they have tended to pursue moderate interventionist strategies. The likelihood of 'crowding out' occurring where there are substantial resources, most notably labour, lying idle is not very significant. Business rates are controversial, but most studies suggest their impact is fairly marginal on local economic activity and employment. It might be noted that a moderate interventionist approach has been endorsed, at least by implication, through some of the initiatives of the Thatcher Government. The continuation of the urban programme, and its reorientation towards economic development tacitly accepts the logic of intervention, while both task forces and the urban development corporations involve substantial direct central government intervention in local economies.

What might be regarded as the mainstream approach to local economic development involves what Hasluck calls the structuralist/ Keynesian perspective, and what Moore describes as a 'modified market' approach. Neither label is perhaps ideal. The implicit rationale behind employment generation policies by local authorities is that the unemployment with which they are faced is essentially structural rather than frictional. The perspective is Keynesian in the sense that it involves intervention without direction, and modified market in the sense that it seeks to correct some of the imperfections of market allocation rather than replace the market. But such labels perhaps suggest a greater level of ideological coherence than actually underlies, even implicitly, many

102

of the initiatives undertaken by a wide range of local authorities of various political hues.

Commonly, local authorities have offered advisory and technical services. The provision of sites, and often purpose-built workshop units and factories, has become widespread. Financial assistance has also been made available in a variety of forms to stimulate new investment or help firms encountering short-term difficulties. A particular emphasis has been laid on assistance to small firms. This partly reflects some disillusion with the benefits derived from devoting resources to attracting large national and multi-national firms, and partly reflects ideologically-tinged assumptions over the intrinsic virtues of small businesses, although more cynically it also reflects the relative poverty of the resources of local government. Special help with training, often in collaboration with the MSC, is commonly available. Many authorities are also now offering wage subsidies to maintain or increase employment (Hasluck 1987).

Such initiatives which would once have been regarded as radical, have become mainstream, and attracted criticism from those committed to radical alternative socialist strategies (Boddy 1984; Mackintosh and Wainwright 1987). Thus it has been suggested that the kind of initiatives widely pursued by local authorities are 'property led, business and market oriented and competitive, with economic development rather than employment the primary focus and with an emphasis on small firms' (Boddy 1984).

It has been suggested that a radical socialist strategy should involve restructuring for labour rather than capital, with the primary focus on employment generation, and with an emphasis on the quality of employment, involving at least a commitment to equal opportunities and health and safety policies and an acceptance of trade unionism on the part of assisted firms, but with a particular concern to encourage alternative forms of business organization such as co-operatives. It has also been urged that a radical strategy should involve the promotion of socially-useful production, which in turn requires a new approach to employment. Such socialist economic strategies were seen as at the heart of the 'local socialism' associated with the new urban left (Gyford 1985; Stoker 1988). They are informed by what Hasluck describes as a 'radical/Marxist perspective', and involve what Moore calls a 'socialised' model of local authority economic intervention.

In practice the rhetoric of 'local socialism' has outrun the reality. One obvious problem is the lack of resources. Radical socialist authorities have had to rely principally on diminishing section 137 funds. The power to spend money on any purpose benefiting the locality, up to the value of a 2 pence rate, as outlined in section 137 of the 1972 Local Government Act, has been the subject of considerable controversy. The

Widdicombe Committee (1986), while endorsing the general principle of section 137, drew attention to the large proportion of this money devoted to one purpose, namely economic development, and suggested that, if central government accepted that this was indeed a legitimate local government function, specific statutory authority for local economic development activities should be given. The findings of the committee underline the current dependence on section 137 money, and the limitations on resourcing local economic initiatives.

Whatever the future of section 137, it seems likely that the financial resources available to employment departments of local authorities for economic development are likely to remain extremely limited. One of the attractions of locally instigated arms-length bodies such as enterprise boards is that they can more legitimately tap additional sources of finance, such as pension funds and private sector money. They are commonly regarded as in the vanguard of the radical socialist approach to local economic development. Hasluck describes them as 'undoubtedly . . . the flagships of local authority interventionist strategy' (Hasluck 1987: 187). But although they differ in organizational form from council employment departments, like Sheffield's, there is little real difference in underlying philosophy, or rather, it might be suggested there are more differences between enterprise boards than there are between this arms-length model and the alternative of direct council provision (Clarke and Cochrane 1988). GLEB, the best known, was also the most radical in conception, involving explicit social as well as commercial objectives and a declared strategy of restructuring for labour rather than capital. The West Midlands Enterprise Board was, by contrast, consciously viewed as a model for a revamped National Enterprise Board, and closely linked with the Labour Party's alternative economic strategy. West Yorkshire Enterprise Board (now Yorkshire Enterprise) has been dubbed Yorkshire's merchant bank.

Whatever their underlying philosophy, both local authority employment departments and arms-length enterprise boards have created relatively few jobs given the scale of the problems faced (Hasluck 1987: 191 and 213). Duncan and Goodwin (1985) have noted that Sheffield employment department created a thousand jobs in three years, a creditable achievement on a small budget and with just thirty staff, but they proceed to compare this with a job loss of 3,000 per month in the city. Similar comparisons could be made elsewhere (see Mackintosh and Wainwright 1987, on the GLC).

Nor despite their explicit social objectives has it been easy to do much for the quality of employment. Inevitably, perhaps, employment departments and enterprise boards have found themselves involved in 'fire brigade exercises' – assisting firms which might otherwise go under, with associated job losses. Market constraints have limited the scope for local planning agreements, and even fundamental requirements on fair wages and conditions of employment have had to be sacrificed in the interests of commercial survival (Mackintosh and Wainwright 1987).

A concern for the quality of work has been most obvious in the considerable assistance which has been forthcoming for worker co-operatives. Forty co-operatives were created in the West Midlands in three years, Sheffield created thirty over the same period, while up to 1985 GLEB had provided assistance to ninety-five co-operatives (Hasluck 1987). Nevertheless, as Hasluck goes on to note, these figures, although impressive, involve relatively modest employment creation. Most of the co-operatives supported are very small, and commonly involve the restructuring of existing business or voluntary organizations. Even so, they represent some of the most interesting and significant projects assisted by local government, and their future will be closely watched.

Support for co-operatives aside, it is easy to detect some disillusionment with the fruits of support for private sector firms, both in terms of job preservation and creation, and the quality of employment. In Sheffield 'employment policy has now switched to concentrate on the public sector – more specifically saving and creating jobs within the council's own workforce' (Duncan and Goodwin 1988: 86). A similar strategy has been embraced in Manchester, and has been advocated on a more general basis by the Centre for Local Economic Strategies (CLES Reports 1987, 1988).

The easiest way that local authorities can expand economic activity and employment in their areas is through direct expansion of their own workforce. The local council is usually by far the largest employer in its area, and the scale of its activities dwarf those of most private sector firms. It follows that the council can significantly affect local employment by reducing or expanding its own labour force. Through the multiplier, council spending on wages and salaries as well as goods and services must have an appreciable effect on local demand and private sector economic activity, although the extent of leakages from the local economy explains why most estimates of the local multiplier are very low.

Such an approach previously had some encouragement at national level. The 1977 white paper suggested that the economic regeneration of the inner cities could not be dependent on special programme money alone, but should involve the bending of main spending programmes to benefit inner-city areas. Such an argument was also taken up by the Church of England report *Faith in the City*, although the latter also significantly pointed out the difficulty for local authorities in pursuing such a strategy in the face of progressive reductions in the rate support grant from central government (Church of England 1985).

Such a strategy now has to contend not only with declining central government financial support, but with legal and financial penalties. It may make considerable economic sense, particularly in those urban areas where the scale of the resources lying idle is sufficient to counter neo-liberal arguments that state intervention 'crowds out' private sector activities (Campbell *et al.* 1987). Yet it is a policy which at the very least requires no opposition from central government, and for full benefits requires the latter's active co-operation. The forced introduction of competitive tendering in several key council services, to be followed in all probability by other services in due course, makes deliberate job creation and an emphasis on better pay and conditions for council employees counter-productive in the services concerned. The net result of such a policy would be the failure of in-house tenders, and the effective privatization of the services concerned, with associated job losses. The replacement of rates by the community charge will also probably make the deliberate expansion of services and employment prohibitively expensive in political, as well as financial, terms, even without the resort to charge-capping, which will replace rate-capping. The conclusion must be that while a co-ordinated programme of deliberate local authority employment creation might make considerable economic sense in neo-Keynesian terms, it requires a radical change of approach at national level, and almost certainly also a change of government for such a programme to have a realistic prospect of achieving its objectives. Heady talk of 'local socialism' can not obscure the basic impossibility of constructing local socialist economies within a national capitalist framework. This is more particularly clear in a situation where local socialist economic development strategies are being actively countered by government-sponsored initiatives with a very different ideological underpinning, and it is to these that we must now turn.

Local economic initiatives inspired by central government

Although we are essentially concerned here with the policies and processes of elected local authorities, any discussion of local economic strategies must take into account the impact of centrally-inspired or directed initiatives, particularly as these are so central to the underlying ideological conflict over approaches to economic regeneration.

Central government intervention to affect the urban economy is scarcely new, although it has markedly changed direction. From the Second World War onwards, it was accepted government policy to discourage new industrial activity in the older urban areas, and encourage the creation of industrial and commercial activity on fresh sites in new and expanded towns well away from the Victorian industrial centres. This policy was implemented through a combination of carrot (such as investment grants and regional employment premium) and stick (the refusal of industrial development certificates, and planning zones).

The character of central government intervention has changed markedly in recent years, in two main respects. First, the policy of deliberately discouraging economic development in the older urban areas has been explicitly reversed. Second, regional policy instruments have been progressively dismantled, with the new emphasis very much on intervention at the micro-level within closely-defined, extremely small geographical areas. Indeed much government intervention now concerns areas which are far smaller than those covered by local authorities, often extending to no more than a local government ward, or even a small area within a local government ward.

Both these developments began before the election of the Thatcher Government, but the second, the concentration on very small areas, has been a particular feature of policy since 1979. The economic rationale for this small area approach has not been extensively developed, although there are clearly some political dividends to be reaped from highly visible transformations of limited areas.

The election of the Thatcher Government has also clearly sharpened the ideological controversies surrounding economic intervention strategies. An administration explicitly committed to the values of the free market, and with a marked suspicion of state intervention in general, and local government intervention in particular, was always likely to cast a very sceptical eye over local authority involvement in economic development. But an ideological presumption against intervention has been substantially modified by pragmatic considerations. A political need to be perceived to be doing something for the inner cities has led not only to experiments with new forms of direct central government intervention, but has also involved the continuation of some co-operation with local government.

Disentangling the underlying ideological assumptions behind central government's various initiatives to stimulate local economic development is at least as difficult as for local government. The continuation of the Urban Programme implies some acceptance of the pluralist or partnership ideal behind the programme. Task forces and city action teams involve a centralist interventionist approach. Urban development corporations are powerful quangos, more symptomatic of Heath-style corporatism than what is usually understood by Thatcherism. They involve a high-profile interventionist approach, characteristic of the flamboyant political style of their instigator,

Michael Heseltine. Urban development grants involve a rather more modest form of state leverage, with the initiation of projects and the bulk of finance being the responsibility of the private sector. Only enterprise zones seem to reflect a commitment to free market values, and even they in practice require extensive hidden subsidies. Thus the Thatcher Government's whole approach to local economic regeneration implies some contradiction of its free market rhetoric, but there are also considerable internal contradictions when particular policy instruments are considered.

While enterprise zones fit fairly comfortably into the economic liberalism associated with Thatcherism, their original conception was the work of the maverick planner, Peter Hall, rather than any New Right ideologue. He suggested the creation, on an experimental basis, of a number of *laissez faire* mini-Hong Kongs in Britain's inner cities with minimum taxation and controls (Hall 1977). For Hall it was almost a despairing anti-planning conception. Everything else had failed, and it would be a valuable experiment to discover how far the deliberate absence of planning could stimulate more new enterprise than previous purposive planning had achieved. The idea was eagerly seized on by economic liberals, however, who had argued for years that high taxation and bureaucratic controls stifled enterprise. The creation of enterprise zones was announced by Geoffrey Howe in his 1980 Budget speech. An initial eleven zones were subsequently expanded to 25 by 1983.

In one sense enterprise zones did not involve a by-passing of local government, as local councils had to bid for them. Yet in another they clearly implied an attack on the principles and practice of local government in general and Labour councils in particular. Firms locating within an enterprise zone enjoy a ten years rates holiday and other tax concessions, as well as streamlined planning procedures. Critics have suggested that the reality behind the rhetoric 'is not laissez faire. It is straightforward subsidy' (Massey 1982).

Judgement on the achievements of the enterprise zones is inevitably heavily conditioned by prior assumptions. There are considerable differences between the experiences of individual zones, which hardly conform to a homogeneous type of area. Most enterprise zones have clearly assisted a marked physical regeneration of the area and stimulated some new economic activity. But they fit the radical criticism of traditional local economic strategies in being essentially property-led. Thus their contribution to job creation is less impressive. Critics suggest that they have assisted a redistribution rather than the creation of employment, in that some firms have relocated within zones to reap the benefits of rates and tax concessions. Moreover, a relatively high proportion of new economic activity attracted into the zones has been in the distributive and transport industries, which are unlikely to provide jobs in sufficient numbers or appropriate to the needs of those previously employed in manufacturing. The long-term prospects for employment, once the initial subsidies are removed are also far from clear. The cost of each job created by the zones is estimated to be at least over £16,000, and could be ten times that if some calculations of their net employment creation are accepted (Hasluck 1987). Hasluck in fact baldly concludes that 'the EZ is really a failed experiment.' At any rate it is not an experiment which the government seems to want to expand, possibly because of the cost.

Urban development corporations have proliferated more slowly than enterprise zones, but now appear to be the government's preferred policy instrument. The first two were established in 1981, in the London Docklands and Merseyside. Five more followed in 1985–6, and a third group, covering relatively smaller areas, was announced for 1987. They are appointed agencies, outside local government control, and substantially funded by central government. Hasluck suggests that they represent 'a market led but managed strategy.' Certainly they involve much more purposive intervention than enterprise zones.

It is difficult to judge the success of UDCs as a whole at this stage, for most of them are recently created, or scarcely past the drawing board stage. The overall verdict on them is thus heavily coloured by the record of the London Docklands Development Corporation (LDCC). In some respects this is impressive. It has revived a relatively large area of derelict and previously virtually unusable land. It has achieved a remarkable physical transformation of the area. It has brought in new private sector capital and stimulated major new investment. Critics suggest that little of this has materially benefitted the original inhabitants of the Docklands (Mackintosh and Wainwright 1987). Indeed the LDDC has involved some explicit social engineering. A deliberate attempt has been made to change the social character of the area by attracting the professional and executive classes through very expensive and exclusive housing schemes and appropriate amenities, such as an airport and recreational facilities. Whether the controversial but considerable achievement of the LDCC can be replicated in provincial older industrial areas remains to be seen. Peter Hall has suggested that the London Docklands location close to the City is a unique advantage, and doubts whether the experiment can be successfully repeated elsewhere (Hall 1984). It may not prove particularly difficult, however, to achieve some show-piece successes from pouring resources into relatively small areas. As a policy tool they may have a more political than economic rationale – as visible symbols of the Government's proclaimed intention to transform the inner cities.

Urban development grants were initiated in 1983. The idea is to use public funds to pump prime the private sector. The projects which have been grant-assisted seem to have been fairly successful in meeting their objectives, but have generated very little extra employment. Moreover, because of the relative paucity of suitable projects, the whole programme has not been able to utilize all the funds earmarked for it (Johnson 1988).

Another central government initiative, the task force, has attracted rather less academic attention, perhaps deservedly. They were the government's highly pragmatic response to the 1981 and subsequent inner-city riots. The first task force was set up in Merseyside in 1983, followed in 1986 by a further ten (officially described as city action teams) elsewhere in the country. Nearly all these initial task force areas had experienced serious riots, although this was less evidently true of eight more which were designated in 1987. Although the initial idea seems to have been the better co-ordination of the work of all the various agencies involved in the inner city, they represented essentially direct central government involvement and a by-passing of local authorities. They were thus headed by civil servants, generally on secondment from their more regular duties. Their impact seems to have been relatively modest. They have concentrated largely on providing employment and training opportunities for those living in the extremely small deprived urban areas with which they are concerned, and on improving inter-community relations. But budgets have been relatively small, some of the projects ill-thought out, and much of their achievement seems more cosmetic than real.

The politics of implementation

Much of the rhetoric surrounding local economic development suggests sharply contrasting underlying ideological assumptions. Yet any more detailed examination of local economic initiatives, whether inspired by local government or central government, suggests rather a tangle of *ad hoc* responses to pressing problems. Specific initiatives have often been announced in haste, subsequently rationalized and sometimes radically redefined, and considerably modified in practice. (See for example McKay and Cox 1978, on the urban programme; and Duncan and Goodwin 1988, on task forces.) Even where the underlying ideological philosophy is clear, as with the Thatcher Government's enterprise zones, or the GLC's economic strategy, implementation has involved concessions to pragmatism. Different agencies working within the same local economic environment are constrained by similar problems.

At one level the debate appears to be between 'local socialism' and the free market solutions of the New Right. However, although quite clearly the advent of the Thatcher Government has polarized thinking on local economic development, the argument has centred less on the merits of state intervention than on the agency for managing that intervention. There is a tacit assumption, albeit reluctant in some quarters, that some form of state intervention is necessary to regenerate urban economies. The question is, who should manage that intervention? Or rather, because the multi-agency nature of local economic development policy would be generally acknowledged, which agency should take the lead role?

Until the advent of the Thatcher Government, that was scarcely an issue. The 1977 White Paper (Cmnd 6845, HMSO,1977) saw local authorities as the natural agencies for local economic regeneration. This merely reaffirmed what was substantially implicit in earlier policy. Although substantial additional central government money had been directed to benefit deprived urban areas, this was channelled through the Urban Programme to local government. Even where the multi-agency nature of policy was explicitly recognized, as in the comprehensive community programmes, where central and local government, other public agencies, and voluntary organizations were supposed to cooperate to produce a co-ordinated approach to the regeneration of specific urban areas, it was in practice the main tier local authority which took the lead role.

The centrality of local government to the regeneration of deprived urban areas was more recently reaffirmed in the Church of England's report *Faith in the City* (1985). The size and scope of local authority operations, their first-hand experience of local economic problems coupled with their developing expertise in dealing with them, and their responsiveness to the local community through the electoral process, all pointed, the report suggested, to a central role for local councils. By then, however, that centrality had been already called into question by a range of initiatives which appeared to involve a deliberate by-passing of local government – enterprise zones, urban development corporations, urban development grants, and task forces (see above).

At the level of political rhetoric, this hostility to local government might seem merely to reflect a general presumption against state intervention, but as we have already seen, the alternatives are also interventionist. More specifically, local authorities have been accused of hostility to the private sector and insensitivity to the needs of business (Walker 1983). Again, there seems to be more in this accusation at the level of rhetoric than in practice. There has been a marked public hostility at times between some radical socialist authorities, like Sheffield, and local chambers of commerce, although this has often concealed a degree of cooperation behind the scenes. Such co-operation is arguably a practical necessity. Local councils act within a capitalist economy and their powers and resources are strictly limited. Even GLEB was forced to operate within the constraints of the market. Local business on the other hand is dependent on services provided by local government. Moreover, the activities of the local council, frequently by far the largest local undertaking, both constrain and provide opportunities for business enterprise. Frequently the cooperation is far from reluctant. Many authorities have enthusiastically entered partnership arrangements with local industry and commerce, and some 300 local enterprise agencies have been established under the umbrella of the Business In The Community initiative (Stoker 1988). So close has been the collaboration of local government and industry in some areas that commentators have plausibly talked of 'local corporatism' (King 1985).

A criticism of local government economic policy which might have rather more substance is that local authorities are too slow, too bureaucratic, and too inflexible to oversee the rapid innovatory development which may be required. This is partly the justification for establishing bodies like the urban development corporations. Critics compare the relative inaction of local councils in the Docklands area with the rapid transformation which has been achieved since the establishment of the LDDC. The councils might reasonably respond that they lacked the resources and powers given to the LDDC. Yet in part it must be acknowledged that the very nature of local authorities as elected bodies accountable to the local community, inhibits some kinds of activity altogether and delays the implementation of others. One of the costs of the democratic process is that full consultation with affected interests takes time. There are bureaucratic delays in local government, but frequently procrastination is caused less by bureaucracy than by democracy. Quick results can be achieved more easily if consultation is non-existent or token. A further point is that if what seems to be required is the physical transformation of the environment to bring in industry, skills, and people from outside the area, rather than provide jobs and services for local inhabitants, this is clearly not a viable political strategy for a council elected by and responsible to local people. This comes back to the fundamental issue of whether policy should be essentially 'place-centred' or 'people-centred'. If the main thrust is towards improving the physical environment, this is a problem for agencies like local authorities which have to be responsive to people.

In practice, despite their handicap as democratic bodies, despite their reputation for bureaucracy and inflexibility, and despite their limited resources and powers, local authorities have been remarkably innovative in the economic development field. A number of independent observers, from the Church of England to the Widdicombe Committee have commented favourably on the range and value of the economic development activities undertaken by local government. The evidence suggests that local authorities and enterprise boards have provided additional jobs at a much lower cost than government-inspired schemes and agencies (Duncan and Goodwin 1985; Bennington 1986; Hasluck 1987). Indeed it is the government's own record in the field of economic development which might appear rather more questionable. Not only have specific initiatives such as enterprise zones proved less cost-effective than local government-sponsored schemes, but central government intervention as a whole has been spasmodic, piecemeal, and uninformed by any coherent purpose (Lawless 1988).

The Thatcher Government's hostility to the economic development activities of local authorities can not easily be explained in terms of either a general ideological presumption against intervention, or local government's hostility to business, or even because the activities are not cost-effective. Partly it reflects a general hostility to local government as it has traditionally operated, and as it has been traditionally conceived. This hostility, and the underlying reasons for it, have been discussed more fully elsewhere in this volume. Whether for pragmatic reasons which might be summarized under the broad heading 'statecraft' or for essentially ideological reasons, the Thatcher administration is moving towards a conception of local government which in future may severely constrain any economic development role for local authorities. If local authorities are in future to be essentially administrative bodies, responsible for a strictly limited range of services, according to strictly commercial criteria, with no redistributive role, it is difficult to see how they can indulge in economic activities which are almost inevitably discriminatory, and which have, and are intended to have, a redistributive impact. Moreover, if the whole scale and scope of local government operations is to be reduced, this will severely restrict the extent of leverage over the local business community and the ability to influence the local economy. Thus the economic development function, while critical to any discussion of the challenge of Thatcherism to local government, can not in the last analysis be isolated from broader questions about the whole future of local government.

References

Bennington, J. (1986) 'Local Economy Strategies: Paradigms For a Planned Economy', *Local Economy*, 1(1).
Blunkett, D. and Green, G. (1983) *Building from the Bottom: the Sheffield experience*, London: Fabian Society, Fabian Tract no 491.
Blunkett, D. and Jackson, K. (1987) *Democracy in Crisis: Town Halls Respond*, London: Hogarth Press.
Boddy, M. (1984) 'Local Economic and Employment Strategies', in M. Boddy and C. Fudge (eds) *Local Socialism*, London: Macmillan.

Campbell, M., Hardy, M., Healey, N., Stead, R., and Sutherland, R.J. (1987) 'The Economics of Local Jobs Plans', *Local Economy*, August.

Chandler, J. A. and Lawless, P. (1985) *Local Authorities and the Creation of Employment*, London: Gower Press.

Church of England (1985) *Faith in the City*, (Report of the Archbishop of Canterbury's Commission on Urban Priority Areas).

Clarke, A. and Cochrane, A. (1987) 'Investing in the Private Sector: the Enterprise Board Experience' in A. Cochrane (ed.) *Developing Local Economic Strategies: Some Issues and Ideas*, Milton Keynes: Open University Press.

CLES (1987) *Economic Sense: Local Jobs Plans*, Manchester: Centre for Local Economic Strategies.

Duncan, S. and Goodwin, M. (1985) 'Local Economic Policies: Local Regeneration or Political Mobilisation?' *Local Government Studies*, 11(6): November/December.

Duncan, S. and Goodwin, M. (1988) *The Local State and Uneven Development*, Cambridge: Polity.

Green, D.G. (1987) *The New Right*, Brighton: Wheatsheaf.

Gyford, J. (1985) *The Politics of Local Socialism*, London: Allen & Unwin.

Hall, P. (1977) 'Green Fields, Grey Areas', Royal Town Planning Institute Annual Conference, June.

Hall, P. (1982) 'Enterprise Zones', *International Journal of Urban and Regional Research*, 6(3).

Hall, P. (1984) 'The Geography of Intervention' in J. Short and A. Kirby (eds) *The Human Geography of Contemporary Britain*, London: Macmillan.

Hambleton, R. (1981) 'Implementing Inner City Policy', *Policy and Politics*, 9.

Hasluck, C. (1987) *Urban Unemployment*, Harlow: Longman.

HMSO (1977) *Policy for the Inner Cities*, Cmnd 6845 London: HMSO.

Johnson, D. (1988) 'An Evaluation of the Urban Development Grant Programme', *Local Economy*, February.

King, R. (1985) 'Corporatism and the Local Economy' in W. Grant (ed.) *The Political Economy of Corporatism*, London: Macmillan.

Lawless, P. (1981) *Britain's Inner Cities*, London: Harper & Row.

Lawless, P. (1988) 'British Inner Urban Policy Post 1979: a Critique', *Policy and Politics*, October.

Mackintosh, M. and Wainwright, H. (eds) (1987) *A Taste of Power: the Politics of Local Economics*, London: Verso.

McKay, D. H. and Cox, A. W. (1978) 'Confusion and Reality in Public Policy: the Case of the British Urban Programme', *Political Studies*, December.

McKay, D. H. and Cox, A. W. (1979) *The Politics of Urban Change*, London: Croom Helm.

Massey, D. (1982) 'Enterprise Zones: a Political Issue', *International Journal of Urban and Regional Research*, 6(3).

Moore, C. (1988) 'Models of Local Authority Economic Policy: Markets and Intervention in Local Economies', Paper given to Political Studies Association Annual Conference, Plymouth, 12–14 April.

Plowden, Lady (1967) Children and their Primary Schools (Report of the
    Central Advisory Council for Education), London: HMSO.
Scarman, Lord (1981) *Enquiry into the Brixton Riots*, London: HMSO.
Sellgren, J. (1987) 'Local Economic Development and Local Initiatives in the
    mid-1980s', *Local Government Studies*, 13(6): November/December.
Solesbury, W. (1986) 'The Dilemmas of Inner City Policy', *Public
    Administration*, 64.
Stoker, G. (1988) *The Politics of Local Government*, London: Macmillan.
Walker, D. (1983) *Municipal Empire*, London: Maurice Temple Smith.
Widdicombe, D. (Chairman) (1986) *The Conduct of Local Authority Business*,
    Cmnd 9797, London: HMSO.

Chapter seven

Race and Thatcherism

Introduction

Local government has been seen as the main vehicle for advancing anti racist politics by those concerned with struggles for racial equality in the 1970s and 1980s. The decade of Thatcherism has, in the main confined the impact of those organizations and individuals involved in the anti-racist movement to the local level. It has been suggested that,

> We must accept for the years immediately ahead, these struggles will be essentially defensive and probably unable to make the transition to a stable, totalising form of politics.
>
> (Gilroy 1987b: 15)

Yet, for precisely the reason that many intermediate race-related reforms have been fought for and won across the terrain of the local state, the practitioners and ideologists of New Right politics have chosen this ground on which to focus their efforts, particularly in the arena of education which will be discussed in due course. These concerns have been forged into popular 'chains of meaning' by the media attacks on 'loony left' councils that have provided the ideological smokescreen and hence popular support for the Thatcherite onslaught on town hall democracy. The intention is to banish 'municipal socialism' from Britain by stripping local councils of their powers over a whole range of functions including local government finance, town and county planning, provision of housing and education, law and order and urban renewal. The blame for the failure of local government has partly rested on the 'loony left' councils and the inspiration for the attack often comes from fictitious anecdotes of the banning of 'Baa Baa Black Sheep' in primary schools and similar tales of the ridiculous.

The purpose of this chapter is to assess the impact of Thatcherism on the struggle for racial equality in local government and more significantly the future impact of the programme of new legislation on black people and popular racism in Britain. The complex nature of

116

inter-relations between local political forces and political institutions
and the lack of necessary connection between economic arenas, political
arenas, and ideologies (Hindess 1980) indicate that there can be no
overall theoretical determination of the impact of local government
legislation, or local government itself, on racism. The analysis of the
specificity of particular policies, struggles, and forces is required.
Racism has been seen to be manifested in the spheres of personal
experience, economic, political, and ideological, legal, cultural, and
aesthetic practice, in fact in most areas of the social totality (Law 1985).
It has been found to be constructed in many independent sites from
which it operates as a structure of oppression with significant effects on
ensuring unequal relations between black and white people.
Disentangling racism from the intermittently rational and incoherent
elements of New Right ideology, where it meshes with ideologies of
culture and nation (Seidel 1986), is a complex process, particularly
where as Gordon and King (1986) and Levitas (1986) have argued the
New Right is made up of a series of competing and, at times, conflicting
interests and groupings. Disentangling racism from the policies, modes
of practice, areas of discretion, procedures and rules of local
government is equally complex, yet the outcome and effects of racial
inequalities and racist actions are clearly and frequently identified
(Ouseley 1981; Brown 1984; Ben-Tovim *et al.* 1986; and monthly
reports in the Runnymede Trust Bulletin).

Thatcherism and racism

Prior to Margaret Thatcher's election victory in 1979 she spoke of the
need to end immigration in order to avoid the effects of being
'swamped' by an alien culture.

> If we went on as we are, then by the end of the century, there
> would be 4 million people of the New Commonwealth or Pakistan
> here. Now, that is an awful lot and I think it means that people are
> really rather afraid that this country might be swamped by people
> with a different culture. And, you know, the British character has
> done so much for democracy, for law, and done so much
> throughout the world, that if there is a fear that it might be
> swamped, people are going to react and be rather hostile to those
> coming in.
>
> (World in Action, Granada, 30 January 1978)

The development of new forms of racist ideology in the 1970s (for
example, 'young black muggers' has been the popular means by which
the riots of 1980 and 1981 were explained) the links between moral
decay, breakdown in law and order, social crisis and young black

117

'hooligans' were crystallized and reflected by the media tabloid press. The attacks by Tory politicians and the media on the purported anti-racist activities of local authorities in the mid-1980s characterized the support for popular racism by the Tory Government. The connection between the increasingly overt racist position being taken by the government and the reduction in voting for the National Front in the general election of 1979 to 0.6 per cent of the total poll and further to 0.1 per cent in 1983 is striking. In 1987 no National Front candidates stood in the general election. The findings of the British Social Attitudes Surveys in 1983 and 1987 (Airey 1984; *Observer* 1987), shows the strength of popular racism as does the regular reports of racial attacks and violence (Searchlight, Runnymede Trust Bulletin). The political legitimacy of the notion of equal opportunities is therefore clearly to be questioned.

The development of anti-discrimination legislation and anti-discrimination initiatives centrally can be described as at best an exercise in 'symbolic politics', as the retreat from the consensus of 'Butskellite' interventionism has led to attacks on the very principles underlying the 1970 Equal Pay Act, the 1975 Sex Discrimination Act and the 1976 Race Relations Act (Jenkins and Solomos 1987). There is a clear lack of support for equal opportunities at senior levels of the civil service and the cabinet, or more specifically for active equal opportunities policies. Passive policies based on equal treatment are propounded in employment by the Cabinet Office and the civil service, whereas equality of outcome or the achievement of equal shares which requires active policies and the pursuit of positive initiatives as outlined in the Race Relations Act 1976 is patently lacking. Civil service policy is primarily restricted to employment issues and fails to refer adequately to service delivery, a massive area of inequality and discrimination (e.g. in social security provision, and even in employment, top posts in the civil service are advertised internally). This, despite being an example of potentially illegal indirect discrimination increases the isolation, stagnation and inefficiency of the civil service.

So, the impact of Thatcherism has been to reinforce and promote popular racism and to undermine and marginalize anti-discriminatory programmes. The impact of this form of politics on the Commission for Racial Equality is a prime example of this process of marginalization. (Appleby and Ellis 1984; Lacey 1984). The question of the high priority concern for the inner cities expressed in Margaret Thatcher's victory speech on winning the 1987 general election requires investigation given her opposition to policies specifically aimed at improving the life-chances of black people who are clearly concentrated in those areas.

The prime motivations for aiming to 'recapture' the inner-cities for the Tories can be summarized in the following way. First, attacks on anti-racism and other equal opportunity initiatives and related attacks on socialism in local government were identified as vote winners; examples of the London effect and therefore the Labour strongholds in urban areas were the key objects of an offensive strategy to secure the continued electoral success of further Tory governments, hence the quote from Margaret Thatcher, 'the inner cities; next time we want them too' (BBC News 1987).

Second, the combined underlying aims were set out of securing political order, social control, and the rule of law and the avoidance of social unrest with its adverse effects on perceptions of political leadership and business activities. (It can be argued conversely that racism and discrimination are bad for business in terms of restricted use of human resources, restricted markets, etc). So, despite the contested notion of equal opportunities and the twin strategy of limited incorporation and marginalization, consideration of equality objectives has been replaced by consideration of electoral and enterprise objectives. Policies for the cities are aimed at promoting enterprise. The DTI's Enterprise Initiative and Action for Cities do not make mention of initiatives or action for equality and the tension between these two objectives is evident in both policy formulation and practice. But, first consideration of the progress of struggles for racial equality in local government is required in order to assess the impact of Thatcherism on black people's opportunities in the future.

Local government and racism

In the last decade under the central control of a Tory Government the political forces of anti-racism have primarily been focused on achieving change at a local level in local government. Indeed as Gilroy has noted this was the period when

> Anti-racism drifted off the streets and into the warm, dry
> atmosphere of municipal buildings
>
> (Gilroy 1987b:10)

But what has this meant in terms of dismantling institutional racism? The overall perception of those involved in attempting to shift local authorities towards the triple goals of equal opportunities, multiculturalism, and anti-racism is the slow and often imperceptible speed of change. The development of race-related programmes, as distinct from intentions and statements has been piecemeal and *ad hoc*.

This process has been heavily dependent upon the effects of a disparate collection of anti-racist forces including anti-racist, community, and campaigning organizations (for a detailed discussion of a framework for analysing local organizations involved in race-related

119

work, see Ben-Tovim *et al*. 1987: ch.4), and those with whom alliances were built, whether councillors, officers, trade-unionists, professionals, clergy, academics or others.

These forces have been ranged against a formidable set of opposing racist ideologies; political, professional, and popular which have led to the general experience of marginalization.

Economic constraints are also evident, where unemployment has been clearly demonstrated to have double the impact on black workers compared to white workers (Department of Employment Gazette 1988) and in the context of 'recessionary politics', re-trenchment and defensiveness have pushed anti-racist issues to a low priority.

As Anwar (1986) has shown the overwhelming electoral choice of black voters is for the Labour Party; in 1979 86 per cent of black voters voted Labour and in 1983, 81 per cent compared to 50 per cent and 43 per cent respectively for white voters. This had led, due to participation by black activists, to the election of four black Labour MPs in the 1987 general election. It has also led to a wider discussion of policy on racism inside and outside the Labour Party and the emergence of the movement for 'black sections' in the Labour Party. Similarly there are now a substantial number of black councillors throughout the country, the majority being Labour members. But as Miles has noted, there is evidence from many commentators (e.g. Fitzgerald, Layton-Henry and Rich 1986; Anwar 1986) that this electoral support arises as much, if no more, from a consciousness of being part of the working class than it does from an awareness of policies which were either expressive of opposed to racism (Miles 1988). Indeed, there is no necessary connection between successful participation in formal political processes and the triple objectives of equal opportunity, anti-racism and multi-culturalism. This link may be stronger and more direct where black councillors or MPs are represented amongst the controlling parties, and not, as with the black Labour MPs, the opposition. Mr. Thatcher has made overtures to the Asian community such as speaking at a rally to commemorate Mrs Gandhi's visit to Britain and visiting Southall as Rich (1986) has noted. For the liberal Conservatives, and for many local Tory parties winning the Asian vote has been a strong issue. Geoffrey Lawler in the Tory Reform Group's journal, *Reformer*, berated the fact that the Conservative share of the Asian vote had increased by only 0.4 per cent by 1983. There were six, unsuccessful, black and Asian Tory candidates in the 1987 general election, and a range of ethnic minority Conservative groups combine in the party's One Nation Forum, and command two seats on the 150 strong executive of the National Union. But the persistent toughness of immigration restriction and expressed racism by the leadership and party representatives despite such factors as the growing number of successful Asian entrepreneurs, will slow the potential increase in Asian Tory voters. The fear of losing Asian voters to the Tories and to the Alliance in the 1983 general election and criticism of the Labour Party's record on race and, hence the disillusionment of black voters, led to high profile commitments on race and repeal of the racist immigration legislation in Labour and Alliance manifestoes. However, as Fitzgerald and Layton-Henry (1986) have shown the 'black vote' argument was massively overstated and they suggest that the predictable response of the parties might be to revert to the previous low profile on 'race' issues, and this comment proved correct in stances taken by political parties in the 1987 election.

Up to the early 1980s black representation on local councils was minimal. The Home Affairs Committee report said that 'it would be a welcome sign of progress if there was an increase in ethnic minority involvement in local politics' and indeed political parties and the process of electoral democracy has been seen as a legitimate site of struggle for black activists (House of Commons 1981). Following the 1982 local council elections, black representation in the London town halls had nearly doubled and 77 out of a total of 1,914 councillors (4 per cent) were black. However, outside London there are very few black people in local government. Senior management in local government departments also fails to reflect a fair representation of black workers. The failure of local government to adequately represent the views of its black ratepayers and taxpayers through electoral democracy through senior officials, and also through general channels of participation, indicates a problem of lack of power and lack of access to power by black people.

In this context local government has been seen as a potential terrain for the expansion and extension of democracy, for 'popular democratic' struggle (Laclau 1977). This can be said to cover three areas of political action as Jessop (1982) has argued. First it involves questions of the formal scope and mechanism of representation and accountability. There are formidable obstacles to the representation of race issues in Britain, due to the political ideologies of race operating in the political parties. Furthermore the institutional separation of the state from the economic domain and civil society ensures that certain key areas remain beyond the scope of formal democratic control and thereby directly available to anti-racist interventions. This has led to the thwarted attempts to develop contract compliance policies in order to develop equal opportunities in the private sector. The loss of a range of functions over the last fifty years from local government to nationalized industries and central government has occurred, thereby leaving a much less localized and in some areas less democratic terrain to struggle in. Second, 'popular democratic' struggle in the local state involves questions of the substantive conditions under which such control can be exercised. The clear subordination of local government to central government which does constrain and change aspects of local government organizations must be emphasized, although there is continuing support for 'localism' and consequently, a debate about central and local relations. Therefore, to move significantly from electoral democracy that avoids issues of black representation and accountability to a wider participative democratic local state would require, at some point, a change in central and local relations. In terms of race, the statutory duty laid on local authorities is section 71 of the Race Relations Act 1976:

> to make appropriate arrangements with a view to securing that their various functions are carried out with due regard to the need to eliminate unlawful racial discrimination and to provide equality of opportunity.

This does provide a condition for popular democratic intervention in this struggle. However, this central constraint has been described as 'general, ambiguous and supported neither by sanctions nor incentives' (Young and Connolley 1981). When the act came into force a joint departmental circular was sent to all local authorities drawing attention to section 71, but no guidance was provided on its interpretation. This guidance has been left to the Commission for Racial Equality and the National Association of Community Relations Councils nationally, and Community Relations Councils and black organizations locally. Further constraints on structural political interventions in the local state may be economic, in that central control of local finance provides a source of conflict and itself a site of struggle in that the resources available for jobs and services may be crucial in determining the scope for significant race interventions (e.g. a positive action training scheme to redress racial inequality in a particular area of work, as allowed under section 37 of the Race Relations Act, 1976). Third, popular democratic struggle over race in the local state involves the interpellation of black people in the democratic rules of the game. Formal democratic institutions do not (and cannot) guarantee that the politics of race in particular will be conducted in a substantially democratic manner, as they could as well provide the means to institute populist, authoritarian government rather than popular democratic government. The development of procedures to ensure black access to decision-making such as working parties or new council committees does not in itself guarantee a commitment to change in policies or practices. This may be dependent on information, political and professional ideologies and personal commitment to the issue which is prepared to temper particular demands in the light of broad anti-racist or equal opportunity objectives. A Policy Studies Institute report found that local authorities had in the main taken little action to directly challenge issues of racism and racial inequality and it concluded that a local authority 'disposition to be explicit about race is a pre-requisite for the development of policies' (Young and Connolley 1981). In other words if local authorities cannot talk directly about racism and related issues they will not move forward, but nevertheless talking does not signify commitment to change and this has proven to be a key factor to be developed, established, and secured in the local politics of race.

Local government has been seen as responsible for playing a significant and direct role in maintaining racial inequalities. Local authorities, often the largest local employers commonly have disproportionately low numbers of black staff. As providers of key services, they frequently provide mono-cultural, inferior opportunities for black and ethnic minority ratepayers. Therefore the immediacy of these issues, the concentration of these communities in the inner cities, the visibility and potential access to local government institutions, have all played their part in leading to pressure from below in the form of demands for equal opportunities, multi-cultural services and freedom from racial harassment. These demands have been pursued through attempts to broaden and extend local democracy and increase participation from disadvantaged groups.

The process of increasing participation in parties and elections, representation on local councils and as symbolic figures (e.g. the mayor of Bradford, Councillor Ajeeb) will help to legitimize the citizenship of black people in Britain and improve their potential access to policy formulation and decision-making. The impact of this process is therefore of potential, rather than immediate, significance. The expectations of such individuals by the communities they represent will be inevitably frustrated by a series of constraints that reproduce, reinforce, and maintain racial injustice in local government. The detailed study, *The Racial Politics of Militant in Liverpool*, gave a useful summary of these constraints identified through the course of political action;

> the colour-blind ideologies of local politicians, whether based on socialist, liberal or conservative principles, which lead to a refusal to adopt positive action measures to redress the balance of proven racial inequalities, or the reluctance to accept the need for special provision to meet particular needs of black and ethnic minority communities; the defensiveness and conservatism of professional council officers which makes them resistant to any serious acknowledgement of well founded charges of overt or institutionalised racism and restrictive of changes to mainstream policies, practices and services in an anti-racist direction; the

protectionism of trade unions which makes them refuse to surrender cherished privileges or traditions even when they are known to discriminate against the black population; the political sectarianism, the paternalistic authoritarianism, the narrow parliamentalist mentality, as well as the sheer crude racism, with which the local council power-elite prove unwilling to genuinely open up local government structures to ongoing black community involvement in decision-making; the smug complacency with which token and cosmetic gestures (an Equal Opportunity logo, a black appointment, a toothless committee, marginal funding for a small project, or anti-racist rhetoric) are used to inhibit the development and implementation of concrete and comprehensive action programmes and policies.

(Liverpool Black Caucus 1986: 137)

These constraints are reproduced throughout local government in Britain. Yet despite these constraints a wide array of intermediate reforms have been made by local authorities, including anti-racist and race equality policies and programmes, ethnic record keeping and monitoring of jobs and services, establishment of race equality targets and timetables, appointment of specialist race relations staff across most local authority departments, equal opportunity clauses in contracts and contract compliance policies, race training, positive action training, racial harassment procedures, and many others. It is not appropriate as Miles (1988) has done to dismiss these initiatives, stating that they have not shown any 'positive consequences for the alleviation of material disadvantage resulting from racism' (Miles 1988). Faced with the challenge of Thatcherism and a dominant ideology held together with notions of racism, culture and nation, as Gilroy (1987) has discussed in *There Ain't No Black in the Union Jack*, the political struggle of black groups and agencies in achieving the changes identified above is in itself a step forward.

The 'riots and uprisings' of the 1980s created a sense of immediacy, urgency, and some political space in which positive race policies could become part of the agenda of local government. The achievements of this process are both ideological and material. As with the increasing number of black councillors, the development of such programmes and initiatives has achieved a foothold of legitimacy for anti-racism in an overall societal context of pro-racism. The creation of barriers to the development of racism in Thatcher's Britain is of prime importance in understanding the verbal and legislative assaults on local government. The importance of the inner cities for ideological and political struggle was not underestimated by these black groups and activists involved in the struggle for racial equality from below. These groups and individuals were also aiming to secure a significant improvement in their material circumstances and conditions of existence which remains the acid test of the 'intermediate' reforms outlined above. Many local authorities including Leeds, Bradford, Lambeth, Brent and others, have to date shown a significant improvement in the number and location of black staff. Ouseley (1981) shows an example of the significant improvement in service delivery, particularly housing provision, which resulted from single-minded pursuit of race equality objectives. The weight of statistical evidence documents persistent racial inequalities in local government but material improvements have been shown to have been made. Indeed the use of the '2 pence rate', locally determined spending used for grant-aid to black and other fringe groups, particularly by the GLC, has led it to become known as the 'political fund' (see *Sunday Times*, 24 July 1983). In Leeds this source of funding was used to finance a £400,000 rolling programme of positive action training for sixty black trainees every two years in career positions within the authority. Such initiatives are under threat and it is the purpose of the next section to review the future for race and local government.

In conclusion, the 'war of manoeuvre' engaged in by these alliances built up in local areas to pursue anti-racist goals, has led to breaches in the defences of local government. This has enabled new forces and new groups to obtain a series of intermediate victories in the sphere of local politics. This form of struggle has always faced the prospect of swift reversal of gains which have been made, and this prospect is considered in the next section.

Two steps forward, three steps back; race and local government in the 1990s

The programme of a new legislation brought in to curb the powers of local government in the period 1988–9 will have a substantial impact on both the development of positive race initiatives and the material conditions of black people in Britain. The purpose of this section is to review the potential impact of these changes.

Community charge

It is true to say that black families in the inner cities will be hardest hit by the community charge. A survey commissioned by the Association of London Authorities reached this conclusion in March 1988. It will not only tend to disenfranchise those hardest hit, by discouraging them from registering to vote but it will force councils to become snoopers in order to collect the tax. Margaret Hodge, chair of the ALA's survey warned

The poll tax is racist in its whole impact. Perhaps that is not the governments intent but it is clearly part of a whole set of policies where any attempt to address issues of inequality does not appear on any political agenda.

(*Guardian*, 3 March 1988)

The main factors determining whether a household will be worse off under the community charge are the size of household, the area in which the household lives and the type of housing occupied. The ALA report showed that black people were found to be worse off under all three headings.

The amount of community charge payable by a particular household is directly determined by the number of persons over 18 living in it. The ALA survey showed that only 4.6 per cent of whites live in households with more than three adults, compared to 10 per cent of Afro-Caribbeans and 13.1 per cent of Asians. Data from the 1981 Census, the 1984 PSI survey, and the 1985 Labour Force Survey all show a significant difference in household size between black and white households. Mrs Hodge also stated that ethnic minority families were vulnerable because their cultural background – particularly Asians – was such that extended families with more than four adults at the same address was common. Despite the ideological promotion of the 'family' by the Tory Government this could be seen as constituting an attack on such values. Using figures produced by the government on the level of community charge likely to be payable in each local authority area, the ALA says, some parts of London and metropolitan areas will have higher charges than average. For example, Manchester will have one of £272, Sheffield one of £248, however Camden will have one of £782, Hackney one of £691, Lambeth £547 and Lewisham £677. The significance of this for black people is that areas where the majority of the black population live where rates are at present low, are precisely those areas where community charge will be particularly high.

The 1985 Labour Force Survey indicated that while 31 per cent of whites live in metropolitan counties and London, 68 per cent of other ethnic groups lived in those areas. In inner London the situation is even more striking, only 4 per cent of the white population live in inner London compared to 21 per cent of ethnic communities, of whom 38 per cent are of West Indian origin.

The type of housing occupied is also a determinant of community charge. The ALA survey found that 50 per cent of white people in inner London live in houses with as rateable value of £250, compared to 67 per cent of Afro-Caribbeans and 61 per cent of all ethnic minorities, which shows an adverse differential impact on black people. Ethnic minorities are disproportionately concentrated in terraced housing (Brown 1984) and will, as a result, be the hardest hit. However, as a study by the chartered surveyors, Fuller Peiser, has shown such people would suffer as much if the present domestic rating system is left unchanged but with a thorough revaluation of property. Occupiers of terraced houses would pay higher rates while families living in detached houses would pay less (Fuller Peiser 1987).

Two further studies by the Child Poverty Action Group and the Low Pay Unit have concurred that those on lower incomes and the poor will be hardest hit. A third of all households would be worse off under the community charge with the biggest losers being those earning £75–£150 per week. The pay differentials of white and black workers are well documented and this is evident amongst those living in houses of lower rateable value. The ALA survey showed that 40 per cent of white households have earnings over £10,400 a year, only 35 per cent of Asian households and 29 per cent of Afro-Caribbean households have this level of income. The survey which has been used to lobby Parliament, found that overall 67 per cent of ethnic minority households in London would lose out compared to 54 per cent in London as a whole. In inner London the impact will be more severe, 92 per cent of ethnic minority households will lose out, the average loss being £759. The report concludes that the prospect

> for increasing racial tensions as a result of this kind of activity is
> obvious, and the result is likely to lead to increased mistrust
> between the black community and the authorities.
>
> (ALA 1988)

Housing

The documentation of the development, dynamics, and durability of racial inequalities in both public sector and private sector housing is a striking feature of the literature on race and the inner city. In the housing field, partly as a result of this research activity, many progressive councils have led the way in developing programmes to ensure equality and fairness in service delivery and also devising ways to tackle racial harassment. Indeed the proposed Racial Harassment Bill which fell at the second reading in the House of Commons in 1985 resulted from activist's concerns about the need to bolster the legislative platform for local authorities in tackling racial harassment. There have been many problems and constraints, not least of which has been an over emphasis on ethnic record-keeping and monitoring of housing allocations, as opposed to placing race and a consideration of the housing needs of black households, centrally in local authorities' Housing Investment Programmes and hence, as an element in decisions on capital expenditure. All these positive initiatives have been threatened by the gradual shut-down of the public sector's house-building role through expenditure controls and the further attack presented in the government's proposals in the Housing Bill published in September 1987. It is no small tribute to the social change Mrs Thatcher has wrought that the Housing Bill in most elements is the received wisdom of all political parties.

Over two thirds of houses in England and Wales are owner-occupied and no other party seriously wishes to do anything except jump on the bandwagon (*Guardian*, 30 September 1987). The bill is a radical attempt to open up the private rented sector and reduce the role of local councils. It fails to mention the growing problem of homelessness and the inequalities and discrimination that face black people in the housing market.

The proposed establishment of Housing Action Trusts and the 'pick-a-landlord' scheme which will give an increased role to housing associations and co-operatives, will in general terms increase the intra-authority barriers to mobility through greater parochial control of housing. For black households predominantly confined to the inner city, this will probably mean that increased discrimination and segregation will result. In the private sector, the abolition of fair rents and increased powers given to landlords will tend to free the market for privately rented homes. More rented housing is required in Britain where the sector has declined from 90 per cent in 1914 to 8 per cent in 1986. This compares poorly to even affluent countries like Switzerland with 80 per cent, and France and West Germany with over 50 per cent. This will occur at the cost of substantial increases in rent and subsequent massive rises in housing benefit. Those in greatest housing need, and there are many indicators, for example overcrowding, quality of housing which show black households in substantially greater housing need than white households (Brown 1984), will see their position worsen. A 1988 report on anti-racism for the private rented sector shows that racism operated by private landlords is rife and that the government proposals will make them worse. Nine large private landlords were contacted, including the Church Commissioners, the Duchy of Cornwall and the Crown Estates Commissioners. The response, received from only three of the nine, showed

> a quite shocking ignorance and complacency towards anti-racism
> and equal opportunities.

> (London Against Racism in Housing 1988)

Education

The hostility of the New Right to anti-racism has been focused on issues in the sphere of education. Anti-racist and multi-cultural initiatives have been identified as denigrating educational standards and as an assault on the traditional virtues of British education to the detriment of white children. Ray Honeyford in a recent debate on television regarding the Burnage report identified four points that were proposed by anti-racists and refuted by the New Right: (i) Britain is a racist society; (ii) white people are racist; (iii) blacks form a separate under-class in British society; (iv) the Empire was bad.

This contested arena has led to a well-publicized string of conflicts in different local areas; the racist writings of Ray Honeyford, a former headteacher in Bradford, the sacking of Mrs McGoldrick, a headteacher in Brent, for alleged racist remarks, the refusal of white parents in Dewsbury to send their children to a school with Asian pupils, the racist killing of Ahmed Ullah in a school playground in Burnage, Manchester and the subsequent report, and the decision in February 1988 of Conservative-controlled Berkshire to scrap the policy on racial equality in education, a policy which represented a vanguard for equal opportunity policies as cited in the Swann Report. In the development of these and other similar events, the placing of issues of anti-racism and multi-culturalism on the agenda of local authorities and schools is evident. In discussing the Swann Report the *Salisbury Review* acknowledges that,

> the veritable revolution in our schools the report recommends is now been implemented.
>
> (*Salisbury Review*, April 1987).

The HM Inspectorate of Schools report on education in the London Borough of Brent, requested by Kenneth Baker the Education Secretary in November 1986, as a result of the McGoldrick affair supported the council's anti-racist policies. The report noted that there is no evidence that the quality of work in Brent schools is being threatened or the curriculum of the schools distorted as as result of anti-sexist and anti-racist policies, indeed such policies were noted as having some 'beneficial effects'. The principal achievement was seen to be its contribution to racial harmony which prevails between pupils in primary and secondary schools. In most of the primary schools there was a 'sensitive response' to ethnic and cultural diversity and the resources and curriculum in these schools reflected the diversity of children's ethnic backgrounds. In secondary schools, syllabuses had benefited from the care and thought which had gone into recasting them so as to affirm the importance of ethnic minority cultures. In a telling passage the report concludes that,

> the Authority's anti-racist policy goes with the grain of local

opinion, has fairly widespread support in the schools and a generally helpful effect on work in classrooms.'

(DES 1987)

The response of Kenneth Baker was hostile, describing the report as 'one of the most disturbing' he had read (*Guardian*, 22 April 1987). A further report by the former chairman of the Commission for Racial Equality, Sir David Lane, into the Development Programme for Racial Equality (DPRE), which relied on the use of £2 million (180 posts) of section 11 funding, and noted the positive contributions made to meeting the needs of ethnic minority pupils. Interestingly Baroness Cox, the prominent right-wing Conservative peer and educationalist has agreed to chair the panel monitoring the work of the DPRE in order to improve its effectiveness. Also, Conservative-controlled Berkshire County Council bowed to a storm of protest over its decision to tear up its anti-racist policy and by April 1988 had agreed to rescind its earlier decision. The policy broke new ground when it was adopted in 1983 by making it a duty for all institutions and services to 'create, maintain and promote racial equality and justice'. Mrs Jean Wallace, Chair of the Multi-Cultural Education Sub-Committee said that the response showed that the anti-racist policy was held in high regard. Black and Asian organizations, teaching unions, headteachers, and religious bodies all opposed the plan to drop the policy. Mullard *et al.* (1983) reported that 36 LEAs out of 105 claimed to have formulated written policy statements on multi-racial education. However, the work of Rex, Troyna, and Naguib (1983) all indicate the limited and partial impact on schools, and Troyna and Ball (1985) have gone further to conclude that 'as change-agents' these policies are not worth the paper they are written on. The promises of 'equality of opportunity' for black pupils through educational qualifications are unrealistic given the present structure of education, and the political dilemma of deciding how minority cultures, languages, religions, and values can be recognized and incorporated into schools remains persistent. The white parents in Dewsbury who refused to send their children to a predominantly Asian school are taking the government to the European Court of Human Rights backed by a right-wing pressure group, the Parental Alliance for Choice in Education (PACE) chaired by the same Baroness Cox. The case in the European Court would, say PACE, centre on whether the government is transgressing the European convention guaranteeing parents the right to have their children educated in conformity with their own religious and political beliefs. It will question whether Headfield, the school at the centre of the row, with 85 per cent Asian pupils, but a 'normal' English curriculum can offer white English pupils such an education. The tendency to polarize local opinions has occurred; a group of white racists chanting 'Headfield' have attacked Asians in Batley, local Asian groups complain of the racism of the white parents and teachers deny their teaching is different from other British schools. The decision of Kirklees Council to give in to the parents' demands signifies lack of political will and the further rolling-back of the minimal gains made in tackling racism in education.

The exercise of parental choice is to be strengthened by the Education Bill and this will increase the problems of racial segregation, racial prejudice, and racial inequality. A Harris poll conducted for London Weekend Television showed that over 40 per cent of white parents believed that it was important for their children to attend a school where most children are from their own racial background. This increased to 52 per cent of parents in the home counties, compared to an average of 17 per cent for Hindu, Sikh and Muslim parents. Baroness Hooper, the under-Secretary of State for Education said,

> if we are offering freedom of choice to parents, we must allow that choice to operate. If it ends up with a segregated system then so be it.

> (*Guardian*, 14 November 1987)

This position and the bill's proposals therefore legitimizes the exercise of choice based on racial prejudice and in line with this, the bill makes no reference to the fact that Britain is a multi-cultural society or the need for local authorities and governing bodies to take sensible measures to reflect the needs of society.

The rejection of schools with a high black presence, whatever the level of achievement and quality of teaching, by white parents combined with the opting-out of predominantly white schools from LEA control to preserve their image and the view that anti-racist and multi-cultural education is irrelevant to their concerns will be a clear trend in the 1990s. On the other hand, mainly black schools, especially where there is a dominant religious group may also opt-out in the growing recognition of the failure of state schools to alter patterns of racial inequality in educational achievement. However, the proposed increase in parental choice, which has given popular support to Tory proposals, belies the reality of unequal choice in the inner city. Poor quality and physical capacity of buildings, differential quality of teaching staff, inequitable distribution of teachers and diminishing resources for education all make the prospect of real choice a myth and an impossibility for deprived black and white people. Also the rejection of notions of multi-cultural Britain and multi-cultural education as recommended by the Swann Report make the proposed national curriculum a failure in equipping all pupils 'for citizenship'.

The strengthening of the power of schools' governing bodies will weaken the implementation of LEA anti-racist and multi-cultural policies and similarly the abolition of Inner London Education Authority (ILEA) is seen as an assault on the policies of equality in education. ILEA, through a hard-fought struggle had come to take a principled stand on racism, giving a high priority to meeting the language needs of pupils, and giving support to community language teaching, access courses, and equal opportunities in employment; its abolition will particularly threaten non-statutory educational provision for black and ethnic minority communities (GLARE 1988b). Ouseley (1988), Gordon (1988), and Francis (1988), all argue that the future will be that of 'equal opportunities lost' and that the New Right will have achieved the increasing marginalization and reversal of anti-racist objectives amongst local education authorities.

Contract compliance

The new 'ideological' politics of local socialism has in some authorities led to the seeking of ways to use the economic power of those councils to promote equal opportunities. Section 71 of the Race Relations Act 1976 lays a duty on local authorities to promote equality of opportunity and it is this positive legislative framework that has enabled such initiatives, although restricted, to weather the onslaught of the Local Government Act 1988. The objective of a contract compliance scheme is not to enforce race relations legislation by excluding 'offending' companies for tendering for contracts although this action is taken as a last resort. Rather, its purpose is to encourage companies by constructive advice and assistance to take practicable steps to eliminate any racial discrimination and to pursue equality targets in employment on a realistic time scale (CRE 1987). The GLC, ILEA, Sheffield, and Lambeth are examples of authorities who have pursued this policy, but the ensuring of compliance is constrained severely by resources and often more basic contract compliance issues like health and safety on building sites. Some authorities like Sheffield have designated their area an 'anti-apartheid zone' and included anti-apartheid restrictions on tenders, suppliers, and contractors. This had led to calls for the banning of contract compliance by employers' organizations. The CBI at its annual conference in July 1987 expressed this view but criticized the Local Government Bill, which will prohibit councils from attaching 'non-commercial' conditions to contracts, for the lack of a specific ban on racial equality clauses being placed in contracts. Trade unions have accused the government of double standards on contract compliance. Jack Dromey, chairman of the local government manual workers union, challenged the government to explain why it was backing a forceful form of contract compliance to combat religious discrimination in

Northern Ireland but making it ineffective on the mainland (*Guardian*, 5 August 1987). Clearly the balance of political forces has determined differing political decisions and the role of local authorities as 'change-agents' is perceived in a contradictory fashion as a result. Objective research by the Institute of Personnel Management revealed that the hostility of contractors to contract compliance was exaggerated and identified three benefits of such policies. First, it was seen as a mechanism for spreading good personnel practice, particularly in the areas of casual and part-time employment. Second, that it made good economic sense to develop fair employment practices. Third, it assisted personnel professionals and others who were trying to raise the profile of equal opportunities in their organizations (IPM 1987). Nicholas Ridley, the Environment Secretary, tabled an amendment to the Local Government Bill in February 1988 to allow a narrow set of ministerially-approved questions to be asked of contractors as part of a council's duty under section 71. Councils will be empowered to include in either a draft contract or a draft tender, provisions relating to the racial composition of the workforce and 'to take this into account in deciding the placement of a contract'.

In September 1988, the Building Employers Confederation took up the potential of this clause by asking for a High Court judicial review of Islington Borough Council's 'non-commercial' criteria in council contracts, asking for a ruling that on twenty separate points, including health and safety and equal opportunities, these contracts fail to comply with the Local Government Act. The answers to these points are used by the council to decide whether companies should go onto the council's approved tendering list. The confederation had complained that Islington were asking for full access to a company's staff records so that a supervising officer could be satisfied that it did not discriminate on grounds of race, sex, disability, age or religious belief.

The majority of job opportunities are in the private sector, about three quarters of black workers are in the private sector and contract compliance provided an opportunity for the success of anti-racist struggles in the local government arena to be extended into the parts that black organizations could not previously reach. The fears of defensive local council members and professionals over the impact of the Local Government Bill in curtailing contract compliance policies has delayed action. Indeed, one of the first actions of Bradford City Council on becoming Tory-controlled in October 1988 was to disband its Employment Services Unit whose role was to pursue contract compliance programmes. But, there is still much to be achieved by committed local authorities in this area despite the government's attempt to undermine this work. Much discussion of local economic strategies has taken place by Labour local authorities and indeed their strategic planning role will become increasingly important as other services are privatized. Yet it remains to be seen whether a race dimension, with equality targets for black workers regionally and nationally, will become an integral part of such programmes. This process is impeded by the statist approach of much anti-racist strategy and new approaches and objectives must be set in order to avoid the stagnation and complacency of the emerging black and anti-racist middle-class elite in local government.

Conclusion

The failure of central and local government and political parties to significantly alter patterns of racial inequality, unemployment, poverty, and homelessness in the inner cities was clear by the end of the 1970s and led to the establishment of new agendas for local government on both the Left and Right. From the Right there has been a drive towards privatization, financial control through cash-limits and rate-capping, efficiency and economy measures, the attempt to replace local government with programmes for local communities decided in Whitehall, and a bewildering variety of government agencies operating in a policy and strategy vacuum, often undemocratic appointed bodies, to supposedly 'cut red tape'. From the Left there has been a drive to merge social and economic programmes, provide training, support job creation, listen and respond to minorities and women's demands for justice and equality, and the extension of public spending programmes.

Local government, however, despite opposing political forces pressing change upon it from below, from within, and from above remains an institution rotten with racism and sexism. The context for institutional racism in local authorities and in the private sector, the voluntary sector and other parts of the public sector is inadequate and ineffective race relations legislation. Anti-racist, race equality, and multi-cultural programmes have so far been largely marginal, symbolic, and cosmetic, at best they have attempted to equalize black people with the level of poverty shared by poor white people. Yet the marginal gains made are being rolled back by the avalanche of Tory legislation aimed at local government which will qualitatively and quantitatively worsen black people's material conditions of existence.

The people of the inner cities need to exercise control over the millions of pounds that go into housing, education and social services, rather than waste energies fighting defensive struggles and in-fighting between different cultural groups and community leaders for the crumbs of additional financial programmes. Financial appraisal of those who benefit from the totality of economic and social investment in urban areas is a key under-researched field that needs investigation. Alliances that have emerged between 'usually excluded' groups of people, and autonomous black political action has been channelled into mechanisms that by-pass the main infrastructure and some black, female or disabled bureaucrats who have been employed to liaise with those groups. The hope that the culture, practices, and services provided by local government would become responsive to the real needs of those groups has remained largely unfulfilled (Ouseley 1988).

The strategy and direction of anti-racist political forces have shown a predominant focus on change in local government. They face the prospect of fighting a defensive war of position, while the terrain on which they are standing collapses, and like Napoleon reaching Moscow, they may find nothing but a shattered structure when taking the reigns of local power in the town halls of Britain. Indeed the problems faced by political leaders with avowed anti-racist objectives in Brent, Lambeth and Liverpool bear witness to this future prospect.

References

Airey, C. (1984) 'Social and Moral Values', in R. Jowell and C. Airey (eds) *British Social Attitudes; the 1984 Report*, Gower Press.

Anwar, M. (1986) *Race and Politics*, London: Tavistock.

Appleby, G. and Ellis, E. (1984) 'Formal investigations; the Commission for Racial Equality and the Equal Opportunities Commission as law enforcement agencies', *Public Law*, Summer: 236–76.

Association of London Authorities (1988) *Black People, Ethnic Minorities and the Poll Tax*, London.

Barker, M. (1981) *The New Racism: Conservatives and the Ideology of the Tribe*, London: Junction Books.

Ben-Tovim, G., Gabriel, J., Law, I.G., and Stredder, K. (1986) *The Local Politics of Race*, London: Macmillan.

Brown, C. (1984) *Black and White in Britain: The Third PSI Survey*, London: Heinemann.

Burney, E. (1988) *Steps to Racial Equality, Positive Action in a Negative Climate*, Runnymede Trust.

Carr, J. (1987) *New Roads to Equality: Contract Compliance for the UK?*, Fabian Society.

Carter, T. (1986) *Shattering Illusions, West Indians in British Politics*, London: Lawrence & Wishart.

CPAG (1988) *A Tax on all the People – the Poll Tax*, London.

Commission for Racial Equality (1983) *Local Government in Scotland*, London.

Commission for Racial Equality (1987) *Principles of Practice for Contract Compliance*, London.

Department of Education and Science (1987) *Educational Provision in the Outer London Borough of Brent: Report by HM Inspector*, London: HMSO.

135

Dieson, D. (1981) 'Thatcher's People: The British Nationality Act', *Journal of Law and Society*, 10: 161–180.

Fitzgerald, M. and Layton-Henry, Z. (1986) 'Opposition Parties and Race Policies, 1979–83' in Z. Layton-Henry and P.B. Rich (eds).

Flew, A. (1984) 'The Race Relations Industry', *Salisbury Review*, Winter: 24–7.

Flew, A. (1987) *Power to the Parents, Reversing Educational Decline*, Sherwood Press.

Francis, M. (1988) 'Issues in the fight against the Education Bill', *Race and Class*, XXIX (3), Winter.

Fuller Peiser (1987) *Domestic Rates: The Significance of No Change*, London.

Gilroy, P. (1987a) *There Ain't No Black in the Union Jack: The Cultural Politics of Race and Nation*, London: Hutchinson.

Gilroy, P. (1987b) *Problems in Anti-Racist Strategy*, Runnymede Trust.

GLARE (1988a) *The Governments Proposals For Education: Responses to Consultation Papers*.

GLARE (1988b) *The Organisation of Education in Inner London*.

GLARE (1988c) *The Housing Bill and Racial Equality*.

Gordon, P. (1988) 'The New Right, race and education', *Race and Class*, XXIX (3), Winter.

Gordon, P. and King, F. (1986) *New Right, New Racism*, London: Searchlight Publications.

Hall, S., Critcher, C., Jefferson, T., Clarke, J., and Roberts, B. (1978) *Policing the Crisis: Mugging, the State and Law and Order*, London: Macmillan.

Hall, S. (1986) 'Gramsci's relevance for the study of race and ethnicity', *Journal of Communications Inquiry*, 10(2).

Hindess, B. (1980) 'Marxism and Parliamentry Democracy', in A. Hunt (ed.) (1980) *Marxism and Democracy*, London: Lawrence & Wishart.

House of Commons Home Affairs Committee (1981) *Racial Disadvantage*, London: HMSO.

Institute of Personnel Management (1987) *Contract Compliance: the U.K. Experience*, London, IPM.

Jenkins, R. and Solomos, J. (1987) *Racism and Equal Opportunity Policies in the 1980s*, Cambridge: Cambridge University Press.

Jessop, B. (1982) *The Capitalist State*, Oxford: Martin Robertson.

Johnson, M., Cross, M., and Parker, R. (1981) 'Ethnic Minorities and the Inner City', unpublished paper presented to Institute of British Geographers Conference.

Lacey, N. (1984) 'A Change in the Right Direction? The CRE Consultative Document!', *Public Law*, Summer: 186–94.

Laclau, E. (1977) *Politics and Ideology in Marxist Theory*, London: New Left Books.

Law, I. G. (1985) 'White Racism and Black Settlement in Liverpool', unpublished Ph.D Thesis, University of Liverpool.

Layton-Henry, Z. and Rich, P.B. (1986) *Race, Government and Politics in Britain*, London: Macmillan.

Levitas, R. (1986) *The Ideology of the New Right*, London: Polity Press.

Liverpool Black Caucus (1986) *The Racial Politics of Militant in Liverpool*,

Runnymede Trust.

London Housing Unit (1988) *Just Homes? The Equal Opportunity Implications of the Housing Bill.*

London Against Racism in Housing (1988) *Anti-Racism and the Private Sector.*

Low Pay Unit (1987) *Pole Axed by the Poll Tax,* London.

Miles, R. (1988) 'Racism, Marxism and British Politics', unpublished paper.

Mullard, C., Bonnick, L., and King, B. (1983) *Racial Policy and Practice – A Letter Survey,* University of London.

Ouseley, H. (1981) *The System* Runnymede Trust.

Ouseley, H. (1984) 'Local Authority Race Initiatives', in M. Boddy and C. Fudge (eds) *Local Socialism,* London: Macmillan.

Ouseley, H. (1988) 'Equal Opportunities Lost', London: *Race and Class,* XXIX (4), Spring.

Rex, J., Troyna, B., and Naguib, M. (1983) 'Development of Multi-Cultural Education in Four LEA's', unpublished report ot the Swann Committee.

Rich, P.B. (1986) *Race and Empire in British Politics,* Cambridge: Cambridge University Press.

Seidel, G. (1986) 'Culture, Nation and "Race" in the British and French New Right,' in R. Levitas (ed.) *The Ideology of the New Right.*

Simpson, A. (1988) *Cuckoos in the Next?: The Role of the Task Forces in Urban Policy,* Nottingham: NDCRC.

Troyna, B. and Ball, W. (1985) 'Styles of LEA Intervention in Multi-Cultural Anti-Racist Education', *Educational Review,* 37(2): 165–73.

Young, K. and Connelly, N. (1981) *Policy and Practice in the Multi-Racial City,* Policy Studies Institute.

137

Chapter eight

Decentralization

Introduction

Much of this book focuses upon particular and substantive policy developments and seeks to identify the ways in which the Thatcherite agenda has sought to mould the way in which policy is constructed and implemented at the local government level. Whether the spotlight is on, for example, local public expenditure or council housing, equal opportunities or economic development, our prime objectives have been to examine the challenge of Thatcherism in each policy area to uncover where such a 'challenge' comes from, and to assess its implications for what local authorities can and should be doing. Such policy questions cannot, of course, easily be examined without reference to the nature of the wider local authority system as a supposedly democratic, responsive and accountable form of community government.

It is to an explicit and direct analysis of the local authority as a system of democratic 'governance', together with the 'governance policies' that stem from Thatcherism and its opponents, that this chapter is directed. Governance policies, to paraphrase Webb and Wistow (1982), are those policies concerned with defining the proper role and remit of local government; the appropriate structuring of relationships between governmental and non-governmental bodies and the organization and management of such bodies.

Reference has already been made to some of the post-war inquiries set up to examine and make recommendation on such matters (see Chapter 2). The argument there was that such changes were mostly concerned with internal organization and process, and that their impact was, at the time, exaggerated. Despite such reforms the essence of the old local government system was retained intact. As Webb and Wistow point out governance policies have been largely an area of taken-for-granted meta-policy during the third of a century following the Second World War. The return of the Conservatives to power in 1979 however provided a watershed; the Thatcher administrations have explicitly sought to bring policies of governance to the centre of their programme (Gamble 1988), and nowhere is this more obvious than in the sphere of local government. This goal has not been approached, it should be noted, through the device of Royal Commissions, or other systematic inquiries or reviews; still less has it been approached through an explicitly articulated and comprehensive reform programme. Rather it has been promoted through a wide range of particular initiatives – like competitive tendering, the community charge, the sale of council housing and other forms of privatization, the abolition of the GLC and the metropolitan county councils, the tightening of central controls over some areas of local discretion (e.g. capital expenditure), and the devolution of powers and controls in other areas (the government of schools and polytechnics).

While such measures are designed to meet quite specific policy objectives, taken together they add up to a paradigm shift in post-war Conservative attitudes to the governance of democratically elected local authorities. They challenge, in fundamental and far reaching ways, many aspects of what we call the 'established' post-war model of local government, and we go on to suggest that they embrace a mixture of 'radical consumerist' and 'competitive pluralist' approaches to reform.

However, the critique of existing practices, and the search for reformist alternatives has not been confined to central and local government supporters of the Thatcherite Right. The Centre and Left of British politics have also voiced significant reservations about the workings of the 'established' local government model and have engaged in widespread experimentation under 'going local' 'community politics', and 'local socialism' banners. These initiatives we suggest, are constructed out of three further reformist tendencies ('decentralism' 'radical democratization' and 'cultural pluralism') and are partly a reaction to Thatcherite policies for local government, but are also grounded in innovative thinking and experimental action that pre-dates 1979.

From all sections of the political landscape, then, there is a questioning of the relations between the principles of local democracy and the functions – regulatory, promotional and direct provision – of local and central government. This questioning addresses fundamental issues concerned with the overall remit of local government: the proper relations between local government and central government and between local government and the public; questions about the nature of effective organisation and sensitive administration; and contested ideas about the proper role of the public service professional.

Questioning the established model

In an important sense the impetus for reform – for example, moving to a slimmed down 'enabling' local authority or promoting a localist, decentralist and community controlled pattern of provision – has its roots in a critical rejection of important elements of the post-war model of local government which has been described as a managerialist admixture of Municipal Toryism and Municipal Labourism. This form of 'bureaucratic paternalism' (Hoggett and Hambleton 1987) reached its apogee in the spate of local government reforms of the mid-1970s and constitutes the point of departure for the reforms of the 1980s. The elements of the established model may be identified as follows:

(i) The expectation that the scope for policy-making by local authorities will be substantially and legitimately constrained by limits set by central government. As we have seen local government has both lost functions, but has also taken on more and more responsibilities. Local government has become big business (Bennington 1975). At the same time it has become more financially dependent on central government and has been increasingly perceived to be the agent of central government. The result is that local government has come to be seen largely a mechanism for the delivery of public services. The continuing process of centralism has been mirrored in a second element of conventional practice.

(ii) The idea that sole responsibility for what remains of policy control at the local level should rest with a council of elected representatives. Council members have become increasingly identified with, and controlled by, a political party machine, and political contest is taken to reflect a distillation of the views and interests of a local population in which significant differences are, with little difficulty aggregated into a two or three party system. Centralized decision-making in local government is reinforced, constitutionally in meetings of the full council and *de facto* through the leadership of a ruling party group which determines agendas and manages business.

(iii) This particular conception of democracy has been complemented by the notion of a bureaucratic administration seen as responsible for both implementing agreed policy as well as offering advice concerning the feasibility of particular policy options. As this 'officer corps' evolved and expanded as new responsibilities were taken on by local government so also there evolved a strong departmental structure – a structure that was only partly challenged by moves in the 1970s towards corporate management.

(iv) These historical trends have led to a further feature – the growth of public sector professions and professionalism. Town and country planning, environmental health and social work have all aspired to and then begun to achieve the characteristics of professionalized occupations (with occupational control over methods of service delivery, over member recruitment and, to some extent, over the definition of consumer needs).

(v) Such features as policy-making by elected councillors, administrative control by a cadre of senior officials, and professionalization of services in a context of diminishing degrees of policy discretion over an expanding system, has resulted in a significant element of local authority centralization. This was seen to reinforce and promote a standardized and impartial approach to provision, to provide some opportunities to reap economies of scale, and to allow the possibility of targeting resources to meet greatest need in the most effective way.

Clearly the elements of the model noted here are presented in a simplistic way and fail to recognize important differences between local authorities, and significant changes that have occurred over time. Thus the steady permeation of party politics has been a long-term process and is far from complete (Gyford 1985), whilst the tensions between departmentalism and corporate management have evolved in different ways in different areas and in different services. Nevertheless this characterization of the 'established model' does point up some features of post-war local government that the reforms of the 1980s have sought to overcome.

The social and political impetus for reform

Pressures for changes in the governance of local authorities is attributed to three linked sets of factors.

Performance appraisal

Challenges to the assumptions of the established model stem in part from a growing body of evidence and assertion about the poor performance of local government – of its failure to 'deliver the goods' in an efficient, sensitive, and cost effective way. From the Right the charge is of wastefulness, inefficiency and profligacy. Ridley (1988) notes,

> Throughout its history, local expenditure and manpower have tended to grow and to consume a large proportion of total public expenditure and of the gross domestic product. Growth has been

141

particularly marked since 1945 . . . . This expansion has placed a growing burden upon the sources of finance for local authority expenditure.

(Ridley 1988: 6)

Unchecked growth and swollen budgets are attributed to the 'blind alley' of post-war collectivist expansion, and the stranglehold that producer interests have had over local government priority-setting.

Whether called bureaucratic paternalism or state-administered socialism (Keane 1988), the bi-partisan collectivism of the post-war years,

> assumed that state power could become the caretaker and
> moderniser of social existence. Intervening in civil society to
> secure the private investment of capital to reduce unemployment
> and to expand welfare opportunities, the state tended to assume an
> omniscience over definitions of citizens' social needs and wants.

(Keane 1988: 4)

Rising budgets and poor value for money has been attributed to the powerful position and special pleading of the expanded local government professional and administrative salariat. Their voice, it is claimed, has drowned out that of the taxpayer and the service consumer (Buchanan 1978).

Furthermore, representative democracy is viewed as a weak mechanism for determining choices about collectively organized provision. As a way of registering such choices an electoral system is seen to be inferior to some other alternatives – most notably the market. An individual has a single vote with which to express a variety of cross-cutting preferences just once every few years, compared with the continuous and multiple-choice system inherent in the market. Further, the free market enables competing choices to be satified concurrently and competition secures value for money (Ridley 1988).

The attack from the Right upon the established model comes, then, from a variety of directions: policy control by elected representatives had been undermined by growing producer power, the capacity of local democracy to act as a sensitive barometer and arbiter of diverse, and often incommensurable consumer choices is questioned, and the capacity of central government to limit and constrain the boundaries of local discretion has been challenged. Their project is not to reform or reconstruct decisional and service administrative structures, but to reassert the supremacy of the individual as consumer and to find modern ways of utilizing the market as both arbiter of contending priorities and as guarantor of cost-effective production of services.

If the Right focuses upon deficiencies that stem from harnessing democracy and collectivism, the Centre and Left attribute the poor performance of local government to two further sets of factors: the pathologies of bureaucracy and professionalism; and the failure to reform a system of democracy that rests on only modest citizen and user participation and, as a consequence, is insensitive in its workings, and lacks substantial public support and legitimacy for its operations.

The argument is that centralized decision-making and political control is found to be unresponsive to local pressures and also tends to put a brake on innovation (Hadley and Hatch 1981). Bureaucratic administration is experienced as alienating and off-putting as well as being subject to the usual types of bureau-pathologies. Professionalism can be disabling and stigmatizing (Wilding 1983) whilst departmentalism is seen too often to frustrate the need for a comprehensive and holistic approach.

Localist remedies build on those anti-statist, yet collectivist views that inspired Guild Socialism earlier this century (Greenleaf 1983). In its modern guise this embraces a concern to achieve new forms of democracy linked to the long-term objective of reconstructing welfare relations (Deacon 1983). Significantly modified power relations between citizens and professionals, and politicians and administrators are envisaged, leading to a new distributional politics. In addition this creates the potential for advances in cultural politics, where more sensitive and finer grained decision-making enables politics to accommodate the growing pluralism in cultural and sexual differences and lifestyles (Boddy and Fudge 1984; Wainwright 1987).

Social and political change

Changes in the cultural and social fabric of British society which help to account for the impetus for reform has been competently analysed by Gyford (HMSO 1986b) in his report for the Widdicombe Enquiry. Gyford identifies two interconnected social trends both of which have influenced changes in public interests and attitudes. According to Gyford from the mid-1960s onwards,

> British political culture with its traditional assumptions of respect for, and trust in, public bodies and of deference towards established authority was showing signs of embracing much more questioning, sceptical and assertive attitudes. Consumers increasingly asserted their rights against providers of goods and services and new commissioners or 'ombudsmen' were set up to respond to public complaints over mal-administration in local and central government and the health service. The onset of economic decline began to mean that questions of how resources should be

distributed became much more hotly contested now that prizes could no longer become available to everybody.

(HMSO 1986b: 107)

Assertiveness refers to a willingness on the part of the public to question and challenge the views and decisions of politicians, public administrators, professionals, and others who make a claim to specialist expertise. The reasons behind this may be attributed to a variety of social forces – the growth of mass education, investigative journalism and a confrontational mass media, direct experience of the 'experts' failures in multi-storey housing, transport design, and town planning as well as the onset of economic decline. Whatever the root causes Gyford echoes other writers who have detected such a trend. Baldock (1977) identified a 'new rebelliousness' in his account of the growth of direct action by community groups, whilst Miliband (1983) used the term 'desubordination' in his discussion of changes in class relations. The implications for local politics are clear – politicians and other groups involved in public service can no longer take for granted a quiescent and malleable public opinion. This is reinforced by a secondary tendency; the growth of a more heterogeneous and segmented social structure characterized by a wide range of cross cutting interests and subcultural differences. Here Gyford draws on those writers who point to the growth of an electorate characterized by more extensive and deep-rooted social and economic differences. Such differences are increasingly difficult to aggregate within traditional two-party adversarial politics.

A largely homogeneous and mass society, in which the dominant social cleavage was based on social class has given way to one that is far more diverse (Gorz 1982; Meiksins-Wood 1986; Lash and Urry 1987). Class loyalties are augmented by a diversity of interests and cultural identifications related to ethnicity, neighbourhood, religious belief, gender, as well as occupation and no occupation. Single issue politics in which pressure group activities and campaigns are seen to cut across traditional political alignments is a further, linked phenomena. The role of politics increasingly becomes one of brokering, facilitating, and arbitrating among contending interests and values rather then one of summoning up some universal 'general will'. The future of traditional representative democracy is thrown into some doubt – its supplementation by a measure of participatory or direct democracy, alongside a substantial devolution of power, being seen by localists as a logical response to such difficulties.

For the Right the response to these difficulties implies a dual strategy. In the first place it involves halting, and then reversing, the ratchet of collectivism and 'socialism'. That is to say fending off responsibility for administering the economy and for deciding the distribution of its product. The respective responsibilities of state and society must be renegotiated. This is both promoted and reinforced by the second aspect of the strategy – the pursuit of policies that re-establish the capacity of state agencies to act decisively and authoritatively.

The social democratic centre and the socialist left must find remedies that enable the continuation of legitimate and manageable forms of collectivism. Here the solutions are sought in the enhancement of sensitive administration (e.g. via decentralism) and in structures that can incorporate and arbitrate competing claims legitimately (e.g. participatory democracy).

Political calculation

The impact of structural and cultural change, and the attendant problems of 'governability' must be attended to – but so also must their electoral consequences. Right-wing analysis suggests that the unpopularity of local government stems from the unfreedoms of collective provision and the profligate spending of empire building bureaucrats. The vast majority of people want a framework which gives them 'choice' in meeting their needs for housing, education or social services. Markets are seen to have a greater potential to generate choice, therefore the aim of local government must be to hive off services to the private sector, to sell off council houses to their tenants and to give parental choice in education. Furthermore in consuming local services people should only pay for what they get. The market is the ultimate form of decentralism. In embracing this model, Conservative Party leaders also argue that this would be of political advantage to their party.

But it was the Liberal Party that was the first to recognize the impact of recent change in British society for political strategy, developing a distinctive 'community politics' in the 1970s (Hain 1976). Party activists permeated and campaigned at neighbourhood and housing estate level, addressing local problems, advocating and politicizing local issues, distributing newsletters and participating in vigorous doorstep electioneering. At their assembly in 1970 the Liberals presented this strategy as a dual approach to politics, enabling ordinary people to develop the skills to redress grievances whilst looking to the Liberal Party 'to break the mould' of British politics. The assembly resolution urged Liberals

> to help people in communities to organise, to take and use power,
> to use our political skills to redress grievances and represent people
> at all levels of the political structure.

Ward and constituency Labour parties responded to localist politics later

– arguing that decentralism was inherent to socialism. However 'local socialism' has been driven as much by pragmatism as ideology. As noted, local government services have not had a good press and services were continuously criticized for their 'alienating' impact. Elements of the Labour Party argued that more locally accessible and accountable services could be more readily defended against attacks from the Right and would at the same time provide Labour with a political campaign to recapture its electoral base.

The responsive local authority: new models and methods

Attempts to move beyond the established model of local authority governance, to a system that is at once more responsive, popular, and legitimate has taken a variety of forms. Such variety, we argue, is constructed out of five elements:

(i) *Radical consumerism* which encompasses efforts to enhance local service accountability and responsiveness through the introduction of market values to institutions and processes within the local government system.

(ii) *Local pluralism* comprises efforts to devolve decisions and resources to local commercial organizations, consumer groups, and non-profit community agencies. Two types of local pluralism are usefully distinguished: competitive pluralism and cultural pluralism. *Competitive pluralism* entails devolution of provision in order to create market or quasi-market conditions (and the benefits that attend choice, competition, etc for service users). *Cultural pluralism* starts from a recognition of the importance of cultural, racial, and other social differences and cleavages that characterize British society, and seeks to devolve provision in a way that promotes maximum sensitivity to such heterogeneity and leads to respect for the integrity of cultural differences.

(iii) *Decentralization* involves the delegation of local government service delivery to area offices (single- or multi-function) in order to enhance user access and increase service responsiveness.

(iv) *Radical democratization* endeavours to set in place additional structures and procedures to enhance popular influence and democratic community control over local provision.

We have already suggested that the Thatcherite Right tends to embrace reforms constructed out of radical consumerism and competitive pluralism while the Left and Centre look to the reform of local authority governance based on decentralist, cultural pluralist, and radical democratic assumptions. Why this should be so becomes clear when we examine each element in rather more detail

Radical consumerism

This element in current reformist thinking and action involves the introduction of a market perspective into relations between state agency and service consumer as well as between state agency and its suppliers. This may be promoted, for example, through the extension of consumer choice in the field of public services, the breakup of producer mono- polies, the introduction of competition and competitive tendering, and through budgetary devolution. Where there is a continuing justification for state provision, the aim becomes one of making that provision more responsive to the demands of users. In addition, because the state too is a consumer of goods and services, so its own purchasing and production operations must also embrace the values of market competition and choice. The persuasive imagery is of the utility maximizing consumer, exercising choice within a competitive free market system. The quest for consumer sovereignty leads away from centralized, and potentially 'monolithic', service providing structures and prompts the search for decentralized and devolved systems.

Such proposals offer not only the benefits of consumer choice, but also help to redefine the ground rules governing 'rational' political and administrative action. Public choice theorists argue that in a variety of ways, the rational and utility maximizing behaviour of politicians, bureaucrats, and voters conspire to promote high spending government (Brittan 1977). The introduction of markets into the internal dynamics of the state sector provides a significant corrective to the 'collectivist' bias.

The Conservative's current approach to reform rests, then, on replacing the monopoly power of the town halls with parallel systems of social provision in education, housing, and welfare. By 'breaking the grip of the town hall', it is anticipated that poor quality provision, unresponsive bureaucracy and the attendant 'dependency culture' will all be abolished. Contemporary proposals for education reform illustrate the model; parents are to have fewer restrictions placed on choice of school for their children (open rolls), within a more diversified system of provision characterized by elements of financial devolution and with opportunities for schools to 'contract out' of local authority control altogether.

Competitive pluralism

Market led 'consumerist' reforms are complemented in right wing initiatives with a distinctive vision of local pluralism. Pluralism, in this context, involves the delegation of local authority tasks and funds to agencies outside the state. These agencies may be commercial organizations; thus in pursuing its obligation to meet the needs of homeless people a local authority may use private hotels and boarding houses to provide emergency bed and breakfast accommodation. Or they may be voluntary or community organizations; local authority social service departments grant aid to voluntary social work agencies, and most local authorities fund community groups (e.g. community associations, advice services, play and youth schemes). Grant-in-aid to the non-state sector by local councils is, of course, far from new. It becomes part of a reform strategy when it evolves into a deliberate and coherent effort to utilize commercial and voluntary organizations to transform the governance of local authorities. Competitive pluralism involves using non-state organizations as part of a strategy to run operations cost effectively and deliver services in a responsive manner, offering an element of consumer choice and service competition.

Central government's most recent reforms in the fields of housing, education, and social services provide examples of this approach (see Chapter 5). Thus in housing

> the government will encourage local authorities to change and develop their housing role. Provision of housing by local authorities as landlords should gradually be diminished and alternative forms of tenure and tenant choice should be increased.
>
> (HMSO 1987: para 1.16)

Opportunities for tenants to transfer to other landlords (housing associations, commercial landlords, tenant co-operatives) is to be widened progressively, thereby increasing consumer choice, giving tenants 'more say', and breaking down the monolithic nature of large estates. The competition integral to such a plural system even benefits those who remain tenants of the council

> Exposing councils to healthy competition should also contribute to a better general standard of services even for tenants who do not transfer.
>
> (HMSO 1987; para 5.10)

Cultural pluralism

This strand of local pluralism involves use of non-state agencies as part of a strategy to both recognize and respond to diversity in local culture, lifestyle, and needs. In this model increased 'sensitivity' and 'respons-iveness' is seen to come less as a consequence of market competition and more as an outcome of the promotion of indigenous community control over local services.

Diverse service users and client groups, sectional and community-wide interests, may all be supported through grant-in-aid and community development approaches in an effort to augment representative democracy with a measure of participatory or 'direct' democracy.

A much publicized example of this approach was to be seen in London during the early 1980s. The central aim of the GLC was described as seeking to 'give power away' (Mackintosh and Wainwright 1987). Almost all council committees disbursed grants to community organisations; in one year (1983-84) to a total of £40 million. Housing and arts projects, technical aid services (to assist groups to draw up development proposals); welfare and legal rights programmes, centres for the unemployed, ethnic minorities, and women – all these, and many other local community initiatives were actively supported.

Glasgow District Council's programme of support to community-based housing associations is another, less publicized but no less interesting example. Nearly thirty associations, covering small areas, employing local people and managed by committees which include local residents, have been used as an instrument in the council's drive to upgrade the city's Victorian tenement blocks. It has been argued (Donnison and Middleton 1987; Stoker 1987) that residents have benefited from being able to express their own preferences through exercising some direct control over the process of rehabilitation.

The rationale for this kind of localist strategy rests upon the value of either promoting, or recognizing diversity. Centralized planning and standardized services are seen to exercise a breaking effect on innovation in policy and practice (Gladstone 1979). Funding and supporting a diverse range of organizations can therefore be used to promote local creativity, inventiveness, and change. At the same time such an approach recognizes, values, and promotes services that can be made relevant to user's particular cultural assumptions and lifestyle preferences.

Decentralization

Under this heading are included all those initiatives that involve decentralization of the delivery, management, and administration of services to a number of sub-authority areas. The areas chosen might be based on ward boundaries, constituency boundaries, or on some other locally determined basis. Variations occur in the number and range of services decentralized (though they often include housing management, personal social services, and environmental health) and in the aims and aspirations of those promoting the reforms (e.g. more sensitive and responsive public services; priority targeting of scarce provision and resources to particular localities). Such initiatives represent an organizational response to perceived deficiencies of the local government system. Once again the aim is to improve the accessibility and sensitivity of local government services; in this case by breaking up monolithic town hall bureaucracy into smaller, locally based, and more user-friendly units.

One of the first authorities to pioneer this approach was Walsall District Council in the West Midlands, which decentralized housing and some other services to thirty-two neighbourhood offices in the early 1980s (Seabrook 1984). Another example, attracting more attention, has been the London Borough of Islington which has decentralized all housing and social services, along with environmental health, street cleaning, and welfare rights to twenty-four neighbourhood offices with each office serving about 7,000 residents (Hodge 1987). Other local authorities to commit themselves to this approach include Manchester, Birmingham, Sheffield, and the London Boroughs of Camden and Greenwich (Hoggett and Hambleton 1987).

This administrative approach to localizing services involves the establishment of a number of neighbourhood based offices each of which operates as a 'one stop' multi-service centre for the surrounding community. There is often an attempt within the neighbourhood offices to move to multi-disciplinary teamwork via the encouragement of new forms of working and the development of an integrated (single status) workforce. There are also some elements of devolved control – administrative and/or financial – from city hall to the local offices. Attempts to liaise with neighbourhood groups, and perhaps incorporate some of them into the service delivery systems is also a common feature. The public tend to be regarded as 'users', 'clients' or recipients of services, entitled to more efficiently delivered, higher quality services, provided in ways that are sensitive to individual and local needs.

Radical democracy

Under this heading can be grouped those attempts to devolve responsible political decision-making to sub-authority assemblies or committees. This strand of localist reform is rarely pursued in isolation from efforts at service decentralization, although it clearly represents a qualitatively distinct – and in many respects a more fundamental – element in any reform effort. There are significant differences in approach to be found in different parts of the UK; some authorities are providing for area committees of councillors, others augment such committees by community representatives; a third option is to institute a network of urban parish councils as a local forum for public debate. The nature, and extent of power devolved from the centre varies considerably, although in the main it remains fairly circumscribed.

Hambleton and Hoggett (1987) have usefully documented a number of recent experiments. An early example was Newcastle's programme of priority area teams (PATs) inaugurated in 1976. There are currently fourteen teams in operation, they are ward based and they each serve populations of about 10,000 people. In line with the overarching aim of targeting resources to localities of greatest need, the PATs have been located in a limited number of multiple-deprived areas in the city. However, with annual budgets of only approximately £40,000 each, the real interest for our purposes lies less in the material impact of the programme than in the success they have had in enhancing local involvement in decision-making about the allocation of funds to local schemes. Each team comprises five key personnel; the three ward councillors, the local county councillor, and a seconded local government officer (the team leader) and it meets monthly in open forum. The extent and quality of public involvement in the deliberations and decision-making of the PATs varies greatly, and seems to be dependent on how far the councillors have made efforts to reach out and get genuinely involved in the affairs of their local community (through liaison with voluntary organizations, participation in local campaigns, increasing information dissemination via provision of newsletters).

A further example of an attempt to extend local representative democracy is the area committee system pioneered in Birmingham. Since 1984 twelve area committees have been in operation, each serving three to four wards (90,000 people approximately). As in Newcastle the committee consists of city and county councillors but also includes the local MP. Originally set up with a remit to monitor the performance of council services there has subsequently been some delegation of powers from the council, although this has happened in a rather piecemeal way which militates against the public being provided with a clear rationale of the committee's role, and why they should be taken seriously. The committees have certainly provided some new opportunities for public dialogue, but with evident limits set by the degree to which attention has been focused on developing operating styles that genuinely facilitate or encourage local involvement. Birmingham City Council sees the area committees as transitional structures, to be superceded by the establishment of ninety parish councils, one for each electoral ward of the city. The aim is to extend democratic opportunities in local government.

Conclusion: community accountability or community development?

How are we to make some general sense of the approaches to local government reform reviewed in this chapter? The five reformist strands are clearly more than temporary fads and enthusiasm; they reflect deep-seated worries about long established traditions of local authority governance. As we have seen, the impetus for change stems from concerns about the past performance record of the system, and of reservations about its capacity to adapt to the changing needs of a changing society. Challenges to the 'bureaucratic paternalism' of local government have now moved beyond questions of internal management and organization (although the approaches to reform discussed here have themselves prompted reviews about internal organization – see for example Widdicombe 1986). These deeper concerns about governance clearly draw significance from being part of a wider debate about the overall role and remit of democratic local government in the late twentieth century.

A key issue – perhaps the key issue – revolves around whether the benefits of local democracy are to be seen primarily in terms of community accountability or of community development. For the Thatcherite Right the urgent need is to enhance the accountability of local government. They point to the poor fit between what people really want, what they are willing to finance, and what they get through the mechanism of local government characterized by lack of political accountability, bureaucracy, and professional interests. Local government has become enlarged and extended beyond its proper remit and role. This is partly fuelled by politicians out-bidding each other in electoral promises and partly derives from the ease with which town halls can be 'hijacked' by unrepresentative factions. Accordingly the solution lies in introducing reforms that ensure community preferences weigh more heavily in decision making processes of local government. Radical consumerism and competitive pluralism are both attempts to to introduce surrogate market mechanisms into local government provision.

Whilst individual choice is central to the reform strategy of the New Right, that of the Left is to create a form of democracy that combines and embraces a social and collectivist vision of local government. For the Right the image of the state is in many respects that of an 'unfortunate' necessity, a set of structures that runs the risk of coercing individual's rights to choose. For the Left the institutional framework of government is perceived in a more benign light; individuals are constituted by political and social organization, as well as acting as the architect and creator of such systems.

It is through participation in the collectivity that men and women individualize themselves and realize their potential, so the form and nature of that collectivity assumes great importance. For participatory democrats the nature of the state (the agency vested with the responsibility for the construction and reconstruction of the institutions of collective life) is thus critical and to extend and deepen the range of democratic practices in other spheres of social life becomes equally important (Barber 1984).

'Going local' by means of the strategies summarized as radical democracy and cultural pluralism thus moves beyond a search for greater accountability. Their real significance lies in the part they are seen to play in a wider strategy of political and community development, one in which the exercise of an enhanced and active conception of citizenship goes hand in hand with collective responsibility for the development of the social framework.

References

Baldock, P. (1977) 'Why Community Action? The Historical Origins of the Radical Trend in British Community Work', *Community Development Journal*, 12(2).

Barber, B. (1984) *Strong Democracy: Participatory Politics for a New Age*, Berkeley: University of California Press.

Bennington, J. (1975) *Local Government Becomes Big Business*, London: DCP.

Boddy, M. and Fudge, C. (eds) (1984) *Local Socialism?*, London: Macmillan.

Brittan, S. (1977) *The Economic Consequences of Democracy*, London: Temple Smith.

Buchanan, J. (1978) *The Economics of Politics*, Institute of Economic Affairs Readings No. 18, West Sussex: Goron Pro-Print.

Deacon, B. (1983) *Social Policy and Socialism*, London: Pluto Press.

Donnison, D. and Middleton, A. (1987) *Regenerating the Inner City: The Glasgow Experience*, London: Routledge & Kegan Paul.

Gamble, A. (1988) *The Free Economy and the Strong State*, Basingstoke: Macmillan.

Gladstone, F.J. (1979) *Voluntary Action in a Changing World*, London: Bedford Square Press.

Gorz, A. (1982) *Farewell to the Working Class*, London: Pluto Press.

Green, D.G. (1987) *The New Right*, Brighton: Wheatsheaf Books.

Greenleaf, W.H. (1983) *The Ideological Heritage*, London: Methuen.

Gyford, J. (1985) 'The Politicization of Local Government' in M. Loughlin, M. Gelfand, and K. Young (eds) *Half a Century of Municipal Decline 1935–1985*, London: Allen & Unwin.

Hadley, R. and Hatch, S. (1981) *Social Welfare and the Failure of the State*, London: Allen & Unwin.

Hain, P. (ed.) (1976) *Community Politics*, London: Calder.

HMSO (1986a) *The Conduct of Local Authority Business: Report of the Committee of Inquiry into the conduct of Local Authority Business* (Chairman David Widdicombe, QC) Cmnd 9797, London: HMSO.

HMSO (1986b) *Research Volume II: The Political Organisation of Local Authorities* (Leach, S. Game, C., Gyford, J.), Cmnd 9798, London: HMSO.

HMSO (1987) *Housing: The Government's Proposals*, Cmnd 214, London: HMSO.

Hodge, M. (1987) 'Central-Local Conflicts: the view from Islington' in P. Hoggett and R. Hambleton.

Hoggett, P. and Hambleton, R. (eds) (1987) *Decentralisation and Democracy*, University of Bristol: Bristol School for Advanced Urban studies.

Keane, J. (1988) *Democracy and Civil Society*, London: Verso.

Lash, S. and Urry, J. (1987) *The End of Organised Capitalism*, Oxford: Polity Press.

Mackintosh, M. and Wainwright, H. (eds) (1987) *A Taste of Power*, London: Verso.

Meiksins-Wood, E. (1986) *The Retreat from Class*, London: Verso.

Miliband, R. (1978) 'A State of Desubordination', *British Journal of Sociology*, 29(4).

Ridley, N. (1988) *The Local Right: Enabling Not Providing*, London: Centre for Policy Studies.

Seabrook, J. (1984) *The Idea of Neighbourhood*, London: Pluto.

Stoker, G. (1987) 'Decentralisation and Local Government', *Social Policy and Administration*, 21(2).

Wainwright, H. (1987) *Labour: A Tale of Two Parties*, London: Hogarth Press.

Webb, A. and Wistow, G. (1982) *Whither State Welfare?*, London: Royal Institute of Public Administration.

Wilding, P. (1983) *Professional Power and Social Welfare*, London: Routledge & Kegan Paul.

Chapter nine

Conclusions: the future of local government

This book has sought to assess the impact of the 'Thatcher Revolution' (Jenkins 1987) on the workings of local government in Britain over the past decade. At the same time it has looked forward, outlining the ways in which local government may be expected to evolve further during the 1990s. In this final chapter an attempt is made to summarize and synthesize the range of arguments that have been developed separately and sequentially within the body of the book, using this opportunity for constructing a simplified model of the politics of Thatcherism as it manifests itself at the local level.

In grossly simplified terms the thread running through the previous chapters suggest that there are two separate and distinct dimensions to the Thatcher phenomenon in the context of local government. The first dimension represents what might be called the 'attempt to construct a new local political order' whilst the other dimension represents 'the attempt to recast the nature of politics and the local political process'. The dimensions are about ends and means; about a vision of the kind of local socio-political system that will best serve Britain in the twenty-first century, and a picture of the most appropriate and legitimate forms of political action to realize such a goal.

Working to construct a new political order refers, then, to the Thatcherite attempt to redraw the boundaries and framework of democratic local government. At its most fundamental it embodies a concerted attempt to redraw the boundaries between state and society and, as such, constitutes nothing less than an attempt to move beyond the vision of society embraced by post-war social democracy. That vision was a long time in the making. As we saw in earlier chapters the late nineteenth century growth of local government was predicated on early ideas of collectivist forms of provision, and involved Tory municipalists accepting the view that the social development of local communities could not be left to the working of the market, to the philanthropy of business, and the good offices of private charities. The

Thatcherite aim of reversing the ratchet of socialism is, in reality, more fundamental still – it is a bid to break with collectivist thought and action altogether.

In process terms the aim is to move politics beyond appeals to 'public interest' and 'One Nation', to a type of politics more fully congruent with individualism and the new philosophy of particularist interests. This chapter uses these two concepts – of the new political order and the new political process – to describe the present and future forms of local government for the 1990s.

Our starting point for examining the impact of Thatcherism has derived from recent interpretations of the workings of the post-war local government system. Many of the studies of local government undertaken in the late 1960s and 1970s, tended to point to the elitist nature of local authority decision-making; that local government offered only limited opportunities for local democratic participation. Elite groups of politicians and local business interests formulated policy outside both the council chamber and the offices of the local authority, and out of reach of any real form of public scrutiny (Saunders 1983). Local government had also become more centralist as local authorities adopted corporate management practices and politicians on the policy and resources committees became the main focus of pressure from local business interests (Cockburn 1977; Simmie 1981).

The Conservatives were not alone, in the late 1970s, in voicing unease about the 'established' model that had developed as a response to this type of elitist politics. As we showed in chapter 8 the established model was associated with profligacy, with forms of expenditure that lacked any real accountability to ratepayers, and for generating local forms of service bureaucracy and professionalism that were unresponsive to local priorities. Local democracy was no longer seen as a strong enough mechanism to guard against these deficiencies. In particular it was argued that those who paid for public services had become progressively disenfranchised, as the linkage between those who benefited from services and those who paid for services had become more and more tenuous.

Keane has characterized this evolution of public welfare provision in Britain after 1945 as state administered socialism:

> the model of state administered socialism . . . assumed that state power could become the caretaker and modernizer of social existence. Intervening in civil society, the state tended to assume an omniscience over definitions of citizens' social needs and wants. Crudely speaking the motto of state administered socialism was 'Rely on the present government and its welfare state

bureaucracies. They know what's best. They'll take care of things for you.'

(Keane 1988: 4)

Keane goes on to note that such a strategy served to generate passivity in the consumption of bureaucratically produced public provision and that this bureaucratically-inspired passivity affected local government in three ways. First, it resulted in a decline of trust in state provision, as consumers experienced the mistakes and 'planning disasters' of the professionals. Second, local government experienced ever increasing difficulty, particularly after 1976, in resolving the tensions created by increasing public expectations on the one hand, and financial constraint and cutbacks on the other. Third, as already noted, local government was seen to have become more corporatist, and less democratic, in its operations; it no longer seemed to act as a neutral broker, arbitrating between conflicting interests, but was increasingly seen to be identified with, and to be working as an agent for, particularist interests.

Thatcherism can be seen as an attempt to confront this passivity, with its associated lack of trust in professional expertise, frustrated expectations, and marginalization of the individual from the local democratic process. The two central elements of the Thatcher revolution become highly relevant to confronting these difficulties. The primary objective, in substantive terms, involves moving away from the principles of collectivism and state provision, and towards individual provision and reliance on the market place. In term of political process and day-to-day political action the objective is to break away from the distinctive and distorted form of One-Nation Conservatism that has characterized the party's politics in the post-war era. The contemporary Conservative disposition must be towards a judicious mixture of the politics of liberalism and individual self-interest.

Constructing a new political order

This objective embraces a number of elements; economic, ideological, governmental, and social. We saw in chapter 4 that the attempt to control local government expenditure derives from the overall economic objective of ensuring that public expenditure becomes a decreasing ratio of national income. The implications of this strategy for housing, education, and the personal social services were discussed in chapter 5. This showed that proposals on grant maintained schools, privatized housing and increased voluntary sector involvement in community care were all predicated on the need to reduce public expenditure. These policies were then reinforced at the ideological level, and we saw how the pressure to redraw the boundaries between private and public sector

157

provision was justified with reference to the values of consumer sovereignty, markets, and public choice theory. Chapter 8 looked at questions of governance and argued that the Thatcher revolution was also associated with a particular form of decentralism, one designed to break with the culture of dependency and bureaucracy. The social dimension, it was argued draws from 'liberal' ideas which put the individual at the centre, and which celebrate the individual's ability to pursue self-interest provided that government constructs a policy framework to encourage maximum freedom of choice.

Thatcherite thinking rests on an assumption that individual and corporate pursuit of self-interest in the market will result in an optimal distribution of resources. Whilst professionals and bureaucrats might be accountable to the elected member of their local authority and individuals have channels through which there can be redress of their grievances, the move towards private sector provision minimizes rather than increases the direct accountability of decision-making bureaucrats and professionals to the individual. Within a market system the only form of accountability available to the individual is to withdraw from the contract and seek another supplier, or to use the process of law and litigation to clarify the contents of the contract entered into within the market.

In shifting existing public services to the private sector the arena of politics becomes that much narrower. Secretaries of State will not have to answer for the public sector if questions are raised in Parliament or in council chambers. Elected MPs and councillors will have no direct responsibility for the provision of services.

Thus the Thatcher revolution is centrally concerned with redefining the boundaries of the 'political'. The history of democracy and accountable government has been the history of ever increasing intervention, either through regulation or the direct provision of services. The expansion of the state has led to even greater expectations of the potential benefits of political action – leading to 'overload', and perhaps even threatening the future viability of democratic government itself. The only solution is to 'roll-back' the state, to transfer responsibility back to the private individual, encouraging the citizen to take charge of his or her own destiny.

Recasting the political process

Chapters 3 and 4 saw that Conservative Party politics has tended to oscillate between what we called One Nation Conservatism and the Politics of Particularism and we went on to suggest that One Nation Conservatism gave rise to a Conservative version of Municipal Collectivism. One Nation Politics represents an attempt to define and promote the public interest, and within the tradition of Municipal Toryism this can take two distinct forms; one suggests that the public interest can be best achieved through voluntary contribution to the commonweal, whilst the other points to the necessity of state involvement. In contrast particularistic politics rests on the promotion of individualism, self-help and self-reliance; the role of government is to construct a framework which facilitates individual self-help.

The politics of particularism tends to advance the short-term expressed interests of electoral majorities. Thus ratepayers' interests (in low taxes) are likely to be given precedence over, for example, improvement in the education facilities of the under-fives. This latter objective is more sympathetically embraced within the values of communal responsibility for the wider community that is part and parcel of the One Nation tradition.

Similarly, local government reform along the the lines of the 'radical consumerist' and 'competitive pluralist' models analysed in chapter 8 are clearly congruent with this particularistic model of politics. Increasing the role of competition, quasi-market mechanisms, and value-for-money criteria in local government all reinforce an instrumental, interest-maximizing approach to political decision-making, and diminishes the scope for considerations of mutuality and responsibility for society as a whole.

The Thatcher revolution signifies a break with the past, in the sense that it represents a highly disintegrating and partisan form of politics; it seeks to turn its back on the politics of social democracy, no longer seeking to provide an organicist approach to government. The priorities of social democracy sought to promote the public interest through state collectivism, including commitments to expanding public welfare and maintaining full employment. Both these objectives were justified as desirable in that they benefited the whole community. In contrast Thatcherism represents an attempt to give priority to particularistic interests, deploying political arithmetics aimed at securing electoral success.

The strategy of political arithmetics rest on a calculation that whilst certain policies may fragment and divide society, the benefits created for certain groups will be sufficient to provide electoral majorities. Thus although unemployment effects 13 per cent of the population the other 87 per cent are still working and are enjoying reductions in personal taxation and increases in earnings. Equally whilst there may be reductions in the value of social security benefits and cut backs in public sector housebuilding, the majority are not dependent on social security or public sector housing.

The reductions in public expenditure and the attempt to achieve most of these reductions through reducing the services provided by local government illustrates the new politics of fragmentation. Local authorities have virtually ceased to build houses whilst their waiting lists have continued to increase. The growth of homelessness and the reliance on bed and breakfast accommodation only effects a minority. This new politics of fragmentation denies therefore that there is one homogeneous welfare state which benefits all; rather, it recognizes there are a plurality of welfare states. There is a welfare state for the homeless, but there is also a welfare state of mortgage tax relief which effects the majority of voters, and which goes virtually unchallenged despite the fact that it benefits those who are better off. Despite the rhetoric of removing the 'dependency culture', a majority of people are still very dependent on government subsidies.

Krieger (1987) has called this form of politics 'the strategy of incompatibles'. It arises when government ceases to pursue the public interest, or act as broker between conflicting interests. The strategy of incompatibles allows for the ascendance of narrow vested interests and encourages particularism as against universalism,

> They artfully forged firm arithmetic pluralities – conglomerate
> constituencies but not unified coalitions – from a set of disparate
> interests and particularistic appeals; on housing, race, anti-labour
> or anti-union sentiments, in defence of the family, or for a fiscal
> rectitude that means privation for the least advantaged . . .
> Nevertheless, manipulation of economic policy has permitted the
> continuation of high risk and divisive strategies based on
> de-integration policies and arithmetic politics.
>
> (Krieger 1987: 194)

The political arithmetic of the community charge shows that gainers from the poll tax tend to live in Conservative areas whilst the losers live in the inner city and other Labour areas. A simple calculation seems to suggest that there is not too much of a political gamble here for the Conservatives although in some marginal seats changes in the poll tax together with the changes in social security might create sufficient losers to make some seats more uncertain. The willingness of Mrs Thatcher, in the 1988 Budget, to increase the amount of savings that pensioners can retain before losing housing benefit shows the amount of fine tuning that goes on in maintaining these arithmetic pluralities.

The political process of fragmentation and disintegration is compatible with Mrs Thatcher's view that there is no such thing as 'society', only individuals and families. Whilst expectations of governments after the Second World War seemed to suggest that policies should be pursued which were broadly in the public interest, the new politics implies that the public interest is a chimera. If it exists at all, it can only be seen as the result of a myriad of individual voluntary actions.

The challenge of Thatcherism and the implications for the future of local government

Our suggestion that the Thatcherite revolution may be summarized in terms of two linked dimensions of change provides us with a model for the further analysis of contemporary, and potential future, developments in local government.

Figure 9.1 offers a diagrammatic representation of the model. The vertical axis represents the Thatcherite attempt to move towards a 'new political order', and the horizontal axis the linked attempt to forge a new concept of 'political action and political process'. The combination of these two axis suggests that there can be a variety of responses to the evolving Thatcherite context. Responses will not be even; the glib generalization that Thatcherism could mean the 'end of local government as we know it' rests on the false assumption that local government can be treated as a homogeneous entity.

We believe it is necessary to start from an altogether different position – that local authorities have evolved in widely differing contexts, have been subject to pressures from a great range of diverse interests, and have deployed their scope for policy autonomy in significantly different ways. The resultant variations in local authority style and policy will not suddenly disappear and we see different responses, therefore, to the Thatcherite challenge. The diagram identifies three variants of the 'post'-Thatcherite Conservative local authority:

(a) *The contract authority* embraces both the changes in political process and political goals identified with the Thatcherite project.

(b) The *business-corporatist authority* will retain a commitment to collectivist values but will be particularistic in its approach to political interests. The wider public interest is to be served, but via the local authority's partnership with the business and commercial sector. The public interest is served through a strong and prosperous local economy.

(c) The *enterprising authority* will explore areas of provision that will generate income through charges for services, and will incline to innovation in the provision of new services through the process of decentralization to community organizations and the voluntary sector. It will take an anti-state approach to provision, then, but will not be highly particularistic in the interests it is seen to serve.

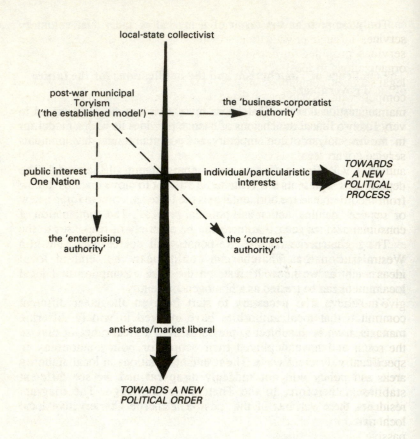

Figure 9.1 Post-Thatcherite local government

Model 1: The contracting local authority

The contracting local authority model of local government is situated in the 'free market, anti-state' and 'politics of particularism' quadrant. It is the 'ideal type' local authority of the post-Thatcher era. The contracting local authority need meet only periodically to look at tenders submitted for services demanded by the authority. Local elections are conducted on broadly the same basis as members of the board of a private sector company are selected. The elected board is responsible to the shareholders – in this case the shareholders are the local electorate. They will look to the return on their investment, which will be the relationship between the level of the community charge and the levels of services received.

The attempt to reverse collectivism and break up local authority services through privatization will have an immediate effect on the services provided in-house by the local authority. Direct labour organizations in local government, faced with overhead costs such as legal services, computing, and capital equipment, will find it difficult to compete with private sector firms involved in street cleaning, building maintenance, and plant repairs. Privatization in these areas is therefore very likely to succeed. The contracting authority will be very vigorous in moving towards free market provision for most local authority services. The legal services department in the contracting of local authority will be expected to sell the expertise of its staff to other departments who in turn will have the choice of purchasing that advice from the private sector. Other departments such as computing services or services dealing with equal opportunities, will also have to find consumers willing to buy their services.

The contracting authority is already taking shape. Wandsworth, Westminster, and Kent, for example, have been spearheading these ideas well before the government introduced legislation compelling local authorities to tender out services. It is likely that the authorities to give the lead will be in the more prosperous parts of Britain where local communities tend to comprise a high proportion of professional and managerial elites, living in modern estates in the towns and villages of the south of England – professionals who are highly mobile with no specific affinity to a local authority. It is hard to see these geographical areas as 'communities' since they tend to lack long-term population stability, community networks and community identification by residents. Residents are likely to perceive their relationship with the local authority as short-term. Their participation in the public sphere is passive and the politicians they elect are equally passive, in the sense that they see their primary aim as keeping down the cost of government. The particularistic interests of these professionals are such that they have little to gain from local authority services; their children are more likely to be educated in the private sector, they tend to be private car owners, and have little use for social services departments or public housing. Privatizing street cleaning or reducing the levels of public transport are hardly likely to lead to major protests.

Within this model of the contracting authority the job of the elected councillor is first and foremost to deliver the annual budget to the various contracting agencies. The link between the voter and the councillor will be confined to holding down expenditure and the level of the community charge.

Model 2: The enterprising local authority

In contrast to the contract authority the enterprising authority, whilst still committed to the new political order of the free market, will differ in its approach to the political process. Whilst the contract authority works on the basis of responding to particularist interests, the enterprising authority remains committed to the political process of public interest, community, and One Nation values.

In the new spirit of enterprise and markets therefore the enterprising authority will reject some of the policies generated by the passive contracting authority. The enterprising councillors will argue that whilst the contracting authority will be providing fewer services, their authority would encourage the development of new services. But these services will be provided by the local authority in conjunction with the voluntary sector and the private sector agencies. The enterprising authority still sees itself as committed to the values of public service but a public service which does not inevitably mean local state provision. The new Bradford Council typifies this form of local authority, in the sense that it has not rejected its commitment to community, with public provision in education and social services. At the same time it is encouraging private sector involvement in for example the establishment of a community technology college for Bradford. Again some of the services provided by the local authority will have to be paid for at the point of delivery. Those paying the community charge will receive free services within the boundaries of the local authority whilst 'outsiders' will be charged for those services. Thus if the enterprising local authority provides some leisure services these will provided 'free' for those who pay the local community charge, whilst outsiders will be charged a fee for using them; equally with library services, parking spaces, museums, and parks. It might be an incentive for some authorities to provide more services which would generate more income and therefore keep down the local community charge. The enterprising local authority could be that local authority which provides more services.

The enterprising authority might well develop new services to attract households to live within their boundary. The enterprising authority which regulates local pollution, which provides parks and good public transport networks will attract those who want to live with clean air and who want to take their children to safe parks. It might attract those social groups who have benefited from the Thatcher revolution; those who can afford high levels of conspicuous consumption but who are also aware that their quality of life depends on collective consumption.

Model 3: the business corporatist authority

There is evidence that in working for a modification of the political process, towards the new politics of particularism, the outcome will be a mobilization of bias towards the interests of the business community. This is the characteristic feature of our third model; the business corporatist variant of Thatcherism combines the political order of the local collectivist state with the political process which promotes local forms of particularism. We would argue that this form of Conservative authority preceded Thatcherism. Saunders' (1983) study of Croydon and Simmie's (1981) findings in Oxford all tended to confirm the 'imperfect competition' that exists within local government. Their argument was that business interests had more access to the council chamber than any other interests within the local authority.

The Thatcher revolution accelerates that trend, especially within those local authorities which find themselves 'blocked in' by previous commitments to public provision. It is the local authority faced with problems like high levels of unemployment and industrial dereliction, and with a community dependent on public transport, social housing, education, and social services that will find this option attractive. The Thatcher revolution legitimizes and gives priority to the interests of business as it this sector of the community which seems to offer a solution to intractable local problems. Some Labour-controlled local authorities find themselves embracing this variant of the Thatcher revolution – Labour councillors in Birmingham and Stoke have, for example, increased their contacts with the local business community arguing that the interests of business and the local community need to be brought into harmony, if economic and social regeneration is to be achieved.

Conclusions: the future of local government

We have argued that an answer to the question 'what future is there for local government?' depends on how we interpret the past. If the interpretation is one which suggests that local government is either the agent of central government or is dominated by local business and political elites, then because this provides little opportunity for local democracy and participation, the changes wrought by the Thatcher revolution will be seen as part of a continuing process of centralization. For those who see local government as a space for local autonomy, local democracy, local innovation and initiatives in policy-making, the Thatcher revolution is seen as a new and rather sinister form of centralism, one concerned with breaking down areas of local resistance.

Both the elite and democratic perspectives on local government tend to be presented as exclusive models. Yet local government can be characterized as both elitist and enjoying a bounded autonomy. Local authorities have always had some space and financial autonomy to give direction in public policy. The history of local government shows that some local authorities spearheaded innovative policies in education, school meals, housing, and public transport, whilst others have been laggards in implementing policy, and have had to be compelled by central government to provide important public services.

Evidence of variations and differences in local public policy tends to confirm the autonomy and political choice of local authorities. Similarly local elections tend to confirm that Britain is not made up of a homogeneous mass expressing similar priorities. Local government and local elections have promoted opportunities for the emergence of different communities of interest.

What makes Thatcherism different is the apparent attempt to deny such variation. The community charge will be qualitatively different from local rates because it will deny the potential for local authorities to fund and develop policy differences. Local government will be denied the potential of income redistribution through the local rates. As Ridley (1988) has pointed out, progressive taxation (i.e. income tax) is a central government instrument; local government exists only to deliver a service.

The Thatcher revolution clearly diminishes and downgrades the importance of politics. When the spheres of politics and democracy are significant to individuals and affect their quality of life a democratic culture develops in which people will value their citizenship and their participation within the public sphere. If politics and democracy are no longer perceived as important, and it is the world of the family, employment, and private consumption which become central, then the public sphere declines. The processes and institutions of local government provided some potential for the expansion of the public sphere. The removal of functions through competitive tendering, grant maintained schools, urban development corporations and housing action trusts by-pass the mechanisms of local accountability and will accelerate the growth of a privatized existence, one in which the atomized individual has little power in any conflict against a centralizing and totalitarian state.

Utilizing the Habermas discourse of the 'life-world', the Thatcher revolution is associated with the ideology of *laissez-faire* as part of a process which legitimizes purposive rationality – a narrow definition of rationality directed towards the choice of the most efficient means for realizing pre-defined goals. It is a form of rationality tied up with increased economic and administrative efficiency (Wellmer 1985).

It could be argued, in contrast, that local government can and must be associated with the life-world; with the world of communicative rationality where the process of democracy, accountability and open discussion seeks to gain some control over and or resist the world of purposive rationality. The world of communicative rationality expresses the desires of individuals and movements. Local government could represent the sphere of the life-world, one saturated by discussion, politics, and conflicts, an arena which seeks to institutionalize freedom through participation and discussion

> However what has happened in the actual history of capitalism is that the forces of system rationalization and system differentiation have proved to be superior to those of communicative rationality. Thus far the counter-forces emerging from the life world have not been able to reverse this trend . . . Today the structures of the life world appear to be increasingly threatened . . . Habermas speaks of a 'colonization of the life world'.
>
> (Wellmer 1985: 55)

The systems world dominated by the steering media of money and power, of science and technology, reproduces a culture of passive acquiescence and reinforces the hegemony of a class of new specialists and business interests. In this context Thatcherism accelerates the colonization of the life world by centralizing and privatizing local government functions.

References

Bernstein, R. (1985) *Habermas and Modernity*, Cambridge: Polity Press.
Boddy, M. and Fudge, C. (1984) *Local Socialism*, Basingstoke: Macmillan.
Buchanan, J. (1978) 'The Economic of Politics', *IEA Readings No 18*, West Sussex: Goran Pro-Print.
Cockburn, C. (1977) *The Local State*, London: Pluto.
Grant, W. (1985) *The Political Economy of Corporatism*, Basingstoke: Macmillan.
Jenkins, P. (1987) *The Thatcher Revolution*, London: Jonathan Cape.
Keane, J. (1988) *Democracy and Civil Society*, London: Verso.
Keegan, W. (1984) *Mrs Thatcher's Economic Experiment*, London: Allen Lane.
Krieger, J. (1987) 'Social Policy in the Age of Reagan and Thatcher, in *Socialist Register*, Kent: Merlin Press.
Manchester City Council (1988) *Contractors Audit*, Manchester Town Hall.
Ridley, N. (1988) *The Local Right: Enabling Not Providing*, London: Centre for Policy Studies.
Saunders, P. (1984) 'Rethinking Local Politics', in M. Buddy and C. Fudge *Local Socialism?*, Basingstoke: Macmillan.

Simmie, J. (1981) *Power, Property and Corporatism*, Basingstoke: Macmillan.
Stoker, G. (1988) *The Politics of Local Government*, Basingstoke: Macmillan.
Wellmer, A. (1985) 'Reason Utopia and the Dialectic of Enlightenment', in R. Bernstein *Habermas and Modernity*, Cambridge: Polity Press.

Index

Index